BORN
TO
SKATE

Also by Edward Z. Epstein

Nonfiction

PORTRAIT OF JENNIFER: A Biography of Jennifer Jones
NOTORIOUS DIVORCES
MIA: The Life of Mia Farrow
PAUL & JOANNE: A Biography of Paul Newman and
    Joanne Woodward
JANE WYMAN: A Biography
THE "IT" GIRL: The Incredible Story of Clara Bow
FOREVER LUCY: The Life of Lucille Ball
LANA: The Public and Private Lives of Miss Turner
REBELS: The Rebel Hero in Films
JUDY

Fiction

THE INCE AFFAIR
AVA: A Play Based on the Life of Ava Gardner

BORN TO
SKATE
The Michelle Kwan Story

Edward Z. Epstein

BALLANTINE BOOKS • NEW YORK

Copyright © 1997 by Edward Z. Epstein

All rights reserved under International and Pan-American Copyright Conventions. Published in the United States by Ballantine Books, a division of Random House, Inc., New York, and simultaneously in Canada by Random House of Canada Limited, Toronto.

Cover photo © AP/Wide World Photos

http://www.randomhouse.com

Library of Congress Catalog Card Number: 97-94234

ISBN 0-345-42136-1

Manufactured in the United States of America

First Edition: November 1997

10 9 8 7 6 5 4 3 2 1

Contents

Acknowledgments

A very special thank you to Chris Kachulis, Laura Klinger, Pat Gaston, Jean Napp, Phyllis Schwartz, Johnny Madden, Joan Perry, Larry and Barbara Eisenberg, and Daniela Gioseffi.

Thank you to all my skating pals over the years—especially to those who graciously shared their thoughts and memories of Michelle Kwan.

For me, figure skating has proven a fabulous, enduring pastime, a wonderful and reliable source of entertainment and pleasure. There's nothing quite as exciting as being out there on the ice; it enables you to expand your creative horizons, stretch your capabilities—and it keeps you out of trouble!

For her memorable performances on ice—and for those yet to come—thank you to Michelle Kwan.

For making this book possible, thank you to Susan Ginsburg, a warm friend as well as a wonderful agent, and to my talented, knowledgeable, and—perhaps most important—enthusiastic editor, Elizabeth Zack.

INTRODUCTION

A Personal Encounter

At a recent postshow evening reception, she looks relaxed and radiant, at ease in her own skin, unruffled by the stir she's causing, and unafraid of the crowd.

"You were thrilling tonight, Michelle!"

"An artist!"

In a sleeveless black scoop-necked top and a calf-length sheath skirt, her shiny black hair falling softly around her shoulders, she is only weeks from her seventeenth birthday.

She has developed into a beautiful young woman. Her luminous gaze is warm, direct, and friendly, her demeanor confident. She knows who she is, she has nothing to hide.

In Madison Square Garden's plush, private, softly lit Club Bar and Grill, many are intent on capturing her interest. Michelle, accustomed to compliments by now, never replies in a phony manner. While others in her position may nod a perfunctory thank you, eyes darting around the room to see who else is there, Michelle Kwan offers her full attention to whoever's speaking to her.

It's obvious she's a person of intelligence and character. Her inner qualities have emerged with dynamic impact on the ice, enabling her to bring a very personal style to her performances. Tonight, appearing in Tom

Collins's Tour of World Figure Skating Champions, she brought down the house skating to "On My Own" from *Les Misérables*.

One knows that Michelle Kwan is holding nothing back: she skates with heart, with directness that artfully combines innocence and maturity. She is totally involved in the art of communication.

While no one can safely predict the future, the feeling is definite that for Michelle Kwan, the best is yet to come.

Edward Z. Epstein
New York City
June 21, 1997

CHAPTER ONE

⁓⊷⊶⁓

Way Up High

This was the moment.

Eyes closed, she lowered her head and clasped her hands tightly as though in prayer. She was deeply focused—this, after all, was the fulfillment of a dream, an incredible adventure.

Here she was, fifteen years old, at the highest level of figure-skating competition. All the discipline and training, dedication and sacrifice had been leading up to this. . . .

Her skates were laced properly, with just the right amount of tension. She knew she must *concentrate, concentrate, concentrate*—focus on one element at a time, mustn't permit herself to be overwhelmed by everything that has to be done. . . .

And she mustn't forget to *breathe*!

Poised to skate her long program in the 1996 World Championships, Michelle was on the ice, standing at the barrier of the rink with her coach, Frank Carroll. They were waiting for the announcer to call her name.

China's nineteen-year-old Chen-Lu, the previous year's world champion, had just delivered a stunning performance, and the judges rewarded her accordingly, including two perfect 6.0s for artistic merit. *Was there still a chance for Michelle to win?*

True, two nights earlier Michelle had won the short program (Chen-Lu was second), but the "short" required less energy, less skating time. It was the strongest short Michelle had ever skated; she had worked "really hard on artistry, every finger, every movement," she later recalled.

And it had paid off—she received first place from seven of the nine judges.

Tonight's long program, however, would count for two-thirds of the final score. In addition to Chen-Lu, Michelle had seventeen-year-old European champion Irina Slutskaya breathing down her neck. In third place, the Russian was a strong favorite with the crowd and the judges.

To Kwan's surprise and dismay, one of her childhood idols, Japanese champion Midori Ito, plagued by health problems and the pressure of competition, had been having a disastrous competition. She fell on her triple axel in the short, and wasn't able to complete a much-simpler jump combination. The former (1989) world champion was in sixth place coming into the long.

Kwan's fellow U.S. teammates, Tara Lipinski and Tonia Kwiatkowski, weren't doing well either. Lipinski, thirteen years old, fell twice and was in twenty-third place after the short. Kwiatkowski, at twenty-five one of the oldest competitors in the event, was in ninth place despite a very good performance. ("Tonia is the crime of the competition. Everyone is appalled," exclaimed former Canadian champion and 1976 Olympic Bronze Medalist Toller Cranston.)

Figure-skating competition—could anyone really figure it out?

Everyone knew that winning the short merely put a skater *in position* to win the event. Many a competitor has won the short and lost the Gold Medal. . . .

That night Michelle was all too aware that a figure skater could never take *anything* for granted—quite the contrary. Every time one stepped onto the ice to compete, one was vulnerable.

Kwan was as finely trained as a fighter pilot, a vibrant young athlete in tune with her body. She felt confident ("Confidence is a fleeting thing—treasure it when you have it," observed former world champion Kurt Browning).

Michelle had proven herself to be a skater with that something extra that could thrill a crowd—provided that tension and nerves didn't sabotage the performance.

"Ladies and gentlemen, representing the United States of America, Michelle Kwan!"

Over the applause, Michelle listened intently to the final few words of instruction and encouragement from Frank Carroll. She'd practiced her program countless times. Performed all the elements successfully. Today was no different—simply a repeat of what she'd done so many times before. Carroll told her that she had to believe in herself, that she could do it. She was one of the best skaters in the world; he knew she could do it. She knew she could, too, and she would!

She nodded in acknowledgment of the applause, relaxed her shoulders, skated to center ice, and assumed her opening stance, in itself a moment of grace and beauty. Her striking costume provided just the right touch of drama and color. The crowd grew silent. Expectant.

For Michelle, *this was the moment.* Would she seize it and make it her own? The seductive opening strains of Miklos Rosza's *Salome* filled the arena as she launched into her program.

A year earlier, Michelle had been perceived in the skating world's corridors of power as too young—"cute," but "still a girl"—to merit serious consideration for world-champion status. So her coach had devised a bold, controversial plan to offset this dilemma: he would present the skater as the biblical femme fatale who performed the Dance of the Seven Veils for King Herod in exchange for the decapitated head of John the Baptist!

Kwan's father, Danny, hadn't been comfortable with this idea—was it seemly for his strictly reared youngest daughter to wear obvious makeup and reveal her midriff? He didn't like to see her put any makeup on at all; in his view, skating was a sport, and he wanted "a sport to be a sport."

But he also wanted his daughter to become a world champion, and reasoned that "she has to become a young lady sometime." However she appeared, Michelle was "still a good citizen and a good student, and that's all I'm concerned about."

Besides, her father knew that Michelle was an intelligent young woman, one who kept things in perspective. She was ripe for the challenge of an image change, and Carroll's plan appealed to her sense of drama.

"When I was little, I always wanted to tell a story with my performances," she recalled. Still, she had found the tale of the seductress Salome somewhat shocking.

Beyond the makeup, the metamorphosis included

sophisticated costuming and coiffure. Michelle's signature ponytail, an emblem of many perky teenagers, had disappeared, her hair swept up into a new sleek head-hugging hairdo.

"It's good to have another 'look.' It's very different for me to play something unusual and exotic," she reasoned. Plus it enabled her to break through her natural reserve, to allow her imagination to ignite, her inner feelings to be expressed through her art.

Her coach had exhibited a sense of humor over the controversy. "Next year, we're doing *The Sound of Music*," he quipped. (In reality, 1997 would produce yet another "exotic" routine.)

For now, her support team was holding its collective breath. Under the scrutiny of a packed arena and nine judges, plus a worldwide television audience, Michelle began the beguiling opening choreography of *Salome*.

It was vital to dramatize emotion, to live through the music—interpret with the line of her body and through subtly theatrical flourishes of her arms, exhibit refinement through technique. *And she must sustain the characterization without sacrificing precision or speed.*

The next four minutes would tell the nerve-racking tale, reveal how world-class skating judges would respond to Michelle's daring new persona—not to mention the complex spin combinations and seven triple jumps she must execute flawlessly.

One fact was certain: once it was over, Michelle Kwan would never view her life or her career in the same way again.

CHAPTER TWO

The Journey Begins

Where do figure-skating champions come from?

Torrance, a residential and manufacturing city in Southern California, is Michelle Kwan's hometown. It lies about fifteen miles south of downtown Los Angeles, and the mild climate is anything but conducive to dreams of ice skating and winter sports.

Michelle's parents, Danny and Estella, have always believed in the sanctity of home and the power of family. Both were raised to believe in a strict, strong work ethic. They were children themselves—Danny around five, Estella three years old—when they first met in Hong Kong, Estella's birthplace. Danny was from the Canton area of mainland China.

A high-energy person, Danny Kwan observed as he matured that especially in America you could become successful in life and achieve goals if you were willing to work hard, learn from mistakes, and never give up. Persevere, no matter what. It was a philosophy that produced results.

About twenty-one years old, Danny arrived in the United States in 1971, Estella in 1975. Their first child,

Ron, was born the following year, sister Karen two years later.

Nineteen-eighty was a memorable year in America. Ronald Reagan was elected president. John Lennon was assassinated. *The Empire Strikes Back,* the second epic in the *Star Wars* trilogy, was released to great acclaim.

It was the year the Kwans welcomed a new addition to their family, Michelle Wing (nicknamed "Little Kwan"), born on July 7. The Kwan children were the family's first native-born Americans. According to friends, the Kwans were a tight family, combining old-world discipline with American directness. Respect for one's elders and uncon-ditional love were givens.

At the age of five, thanks to brother Ron, Michelle took her first steps on the ice at a local mall rink. Observ-ing Ron play hockey, both Karen and Michelle expressed a desire to skate.

It's fascinating to observe young children on the ice. When their ankles turn in, it is assumed "weak ankles" are the cause. In fact, improper equipment is responsible (this is true of adults as well); there is not enough support in cheaply made or well-worn boots. Talent is a real question, but "weak ankles" are a fallacy.

Many youngsters are fearful and tentative on the ice. They don't seem to have a natural sense of balance. They're terrified and relieved when the skating session is over (assuming they remain for its entirety). Cries of "I want to go home!" often echo through both the damp atmosphere of indoor rinks and the crisp air of outdoor ponds.

For other children, being out on the ice is a source of great pleasure and joy from the start. *I like this! I want to do this!* Immediately there will be attempts to spin on two feet, sometimes on one foot! They've seen it on television—it looks so easy! They fall, but determinedly try again.

They reach out for a mentor. "How do you do a spin?" "Can you teach me to jump?" They will *try*, no matter the consequences, and are eager for the next session.

Little Michelle and Karen were happy on the ice. But there was no rush to buy equipment—skates were rented for the girls.

There are many examples of parents who push a youngster, who need to achieve success through their children. Then there are youngsters who badger their parents, anxious to pursue a pastime with all their heart and soul.

(Years ago, one overweight boy from Englewood, New Jersey, was determined to skate no matter *who* told him he was wasting his time. So began the skating career of Richard ["Dick"] Button, who later jumped the first double axel and triple loop in competition, and who invented the flying-camel spin, originally called the "Button camel." The boy who had been advised not to take up skating wound up winning seven U.S. Nationals [1946–1952], two Olympic Gold Medals [1948 and 1952], and five consecutive World Championships.)

Michelle was fearless and adventurous, and her natural ability was soon obvious. Her desire to skate was intense, and her parents recognized it.

Energetic, adorable, and gifted, Michelle resembled a tiny F. A. O. Schwarz doll on the ice. She grasped a key concept: how to skate swiftly and confidently on the edges of her blades, not fearful of leaning deeply into her edges, forward and backward, when she stroked around the rink.

Michelle was obedient, determined, eager, and willing to work hard. She *enjoyed* skating; it was not an ordeal to be endured to please someone else. She "had a good attitude," an invaluable asset in a competitive world in any field.

And her parents had a good attitude, too, approaching the situation correctly. Their attitude was, in effect: "You can't live through your kids, you have to live *for* them."

Many of Michelle's peers in other fields have experienced the same unconditional support from family. "Our parents didn't push us into this," said eleven-year-old Zachary Hanson, who is one third (along with brother Taylor, thirteen, and Isaac, sixteen) of the hit singing group Hanson. "This [career] was *our* thing. But they helped us with it. They said, 'I'm going to drive you to where you want to go and get you what you need.' "

At the age of seven and a half, Michelle skated in her first competition. Her approach was a simple one: just go out there and skate. She has remembered with amusement how, on one occasion, when her name was called, she skated out onto the ice . . . and promptly fell!

Danny Kwan and his wife were determined to do their best to encourage and support their little daughter's dream. After all, it was a healthy pastime—and physical fitness and a good mind go together.

Michelle quickly learned all the single jumps, such as the basic "waltz jump," where the skater steps forward onto an outside edge and leaps a half turn in the air, landing on the opposite foot on a back outside edge (it looked more like a hop at such an early age).

The waltz jump is the basis for the "axel," which has the same takeoff and landing . . . only with one and a half revolutions in the air.

Decades ago, the axel, named for its Norwegian creator, Axel Paulsen, was the most difficult jump in figure skating. It can be treacherous and risky; the only jump done from a forward outside-edge takeoff, one can catch the blade's toe pick on takeoff and plummet down onto the ice face first.

Some budding skaters are never able to execute this basic move comfortably. Michelle mastered it and was eager to move on, although of all the jumps, the most difficult for her to learn would be the double axel.

Her favorite jump was the "lutz," named for its Austrian creator, Alois Lutz. Skating on a back outside edge, one has to reach back with the free leg and, with the toe pick, vault oneself into the air, do a complete counterclockwise turn, and land on the opposite foot, on a back outside edge.

Michelle would later declare that there wasn't anything she didn't like about skating. She found it fun and exciting.

Figure skating is a very expensive sport and money wasn't plentiful in the Kwan household. Lessons, ice time, boots, blades, and outfits were only part of the commitment. If Michelle's interest went further, travel and living expenses would enter the picture and cost a fortune ($50,000 a year is not unusual). One parent would have to be with the child at virtually all times; undertaking a skating career is a deep family commitment.

A "let's be practical and see what happens" approach

prevailed in the Kwan family, and Michelle continued in public school. In Torrance, there was a Kwan family business—a Chinese restaurant, the Golden Pheasant. It was owned by Michelle's grandparents and managed by her mom ("Mum"), Estella. Danny Kwan was a supervisor and systems analyst for Pacific Bell. With cautious resolve, the Kwans contemplated a decision about their daughter's future on the ice.

The odds for a skating career were hardly in Michelle's favor: they're not in *anybody*'s favor. After all, how many figure skaters make it to the top? Perhaps one in one hundred thousand? One in a million?

But who would be the one to quash Michelle's dream? After all, *maybe she'll be that one. . . .*

An important plus in Michelle's life was her elegant, taller, older sister, Karen. The sisters were close to each other and had each other to turn to for comfort and support in times of stress. They were close friends as well as sisters, and over the years would train together and sometimes skate in the same competitions.

How did Michelle feel about that? She said both she and Karen tried to do their best, and if either one didn't skate well, they'd just tell each other that they were having a bad day and to keep on going. They always wished each other "good luck" and one never told the other she'd skated badly.

Danny Kwan, close to all his children, was fiercely protective of his daughters. "I always talk about life with them," he once explained. "I tell them life isn't fair. Some people are born pretty, some aren't. You take whatever you get and learn to be satisfied. The bottom line is, what my wife and I expect from them is not a Gold Medal, but for them to have a happy life always."

At the time Michelle began skating, in the mid-1980s, what are called "school figures" were still an essential element in competition. No one could become a champion without mastering the art of figures. "Why not just eliminate them?" complained many skaters over the years, and even, on occasion, coaches and officials.

By the time you reached the senior level of competition, and passed all eight figure-skating tests (becoming a "Gold Medalist"), you had learned literally dozens of figures. These were figure-eight patterns of varying sizes and configurations, which had to be traced and retraced until the ice looked as though a calligrapher had been at work. Each figure was skated on both the right and left foot, on an outside and then an inside edge, then forward and backward.

A competitive skater had to rise before dawn and travel to the rink for an early-morning "patch"—a clear strip of ice, running half the width of the rink, portioned off to each skater, on which she practiced school figures.

At one time school figures had a value of 60 percent in deciding final competitive standings, and had little to do with the skating the public saw—"free skating," or the jumps, spins, and choreography that characterize a skater's performance. Paradoxical though it sounds, it was possible to be a genius at school figures and mediocre in the free skate . . . and still win the competition!

Also by the time Michelle was in the game, if a skater couldn't do triple jumps, he or she could forget about competition. Skating had become a "jumping" contest, and the future offered no indication of change.

If anything, things were getting worse: the more revolutions in the air, the better. Skaters were already attempting a "quad," *four* turns in the air. School figures were on the verge of obsolescence; it was only a matter of time before they would be phased out completely.

Michelle and her family often watched the major competitions on television. Ever since she was small, she'd said things like, "Wouldn't it be weird if *I* became world champion?"

Teenager Tiffany Chin, a precocious prodigy of Asian descent, had won both great acclaim and the U.S. Senior Ladies' Championship in 1985 (Debi Thomas and Caryn Kadavy placed second and third, respectively). Chin was expected to scale the heights, especially after she placed third in the Worlds that year and the media enthused about her delicate grace and powerful jumps.

But fortunes change without warning in the slippery world of figure skating. Chin, the next year, dropped to third in the Nationals (Debi Thomas won, the first black champion in the history of figure skating; Kadavy placed second). Chin managed to place third again at the Worlds.

Still, Chin's mom had made her presence known throughout her daughter's career. In some circles, she was regarded as an overbearing "stage mother." Tiffany Chin, a future UCLA graduate, disagreed—her mother had simply watched out scrupulously for her best interests.

For maintaining a successful competitive career without enthusiastic family support is virtually impossible. Even Peggy Fleming, America's soft-spoken ice princess of the sixties and seventies, the "Audrey Hepburn of Figure Skaters," as she has been called, had the benefit of a feared and respected "stage mom."

As a father, Danny Kwan was not unlike Tiger Woods's dad. Tiger, a prodigy on the golf course the way Michelle was to become on the ice, has affectionately described his father, a burly ex-marine, as "a pretty tough dog." It is a description that could apply to the slim, youthful-looking, bespectacled Danny Kwan as well.

Michelle was taught that mental focus was the key—*she* was in charge, and it was her fault if she permitted her focus to wander. She must make her choices in life carefully. Life isn't fair; no reason to expect the skating world to be fair, so *be prepared*—thorough preparation makes its own luck.

Vital and alive in the Kwan household was a sense of mutual respect and belief in the values espoused by successful achievers. *Opportunities are plentiful for those who are prepared for them. The difference between the impossible and the possible lies in a person's determination. There are no shortcuts to any place worth going.*

Michelle was taught to have confidence in herself, to develop a sense of who she was. And she was also taught that she mustn't limit herself; she was encouraged to go ahead, be creative!

She was protected, doted on, appreciated. All this gave Michelle an edge.

Michelle got a big kick out of watching Brian Boitano on television when he won the 1988 Olympics. Boitano was a sensational jumper, and his expertise made a big impression on the eight-year-old. To her, the Olympics seemed like the place to be. No problem, she thought, I'll go to the Olympics.

Family friend Bob Clay has recalled, "The Olympics has been [Michelle's] dream ever since she watched Brian Boitano on TV skating in the Olympics. She immediately decided she wanted to be like him. Her family taped Brian's Olympics and Michelle has watched it a billion times."

When Michelle was nine, several fast-rising stars in the skating world were of particular interest to the Kwans. One that held special importance was Kristi Yamaguchi, a seventeen-year-old American beauty, a skater of exceptional grace and power.

Unlike Michelle, who was on the ice by age five, Kristi had to wear special corrective shoes and plaster casts on her feet until she was six years old in order to correct a defect. Her father, Jim, a dentist, and her mother, Carole, had urged her to skate in the interests of strengthening her feet. Like the Kwans and so many others, the Yamaguchis had a tough time paying the skating bills. But Kristi developed into the girl with the "golden feet." She became that one in a million.

Midori Ito, the Japanese champion, was very athletic and capable of huge jumps equal to any man's in height and distance. Midori was another skater Michelle observed closely on TV. She admired many skaters, and later said that if somebody did something she liked, she remembered it for possible future use.

Ito was successfully landing the triple axel, comprising three and a half revolutions in the air. It was the most difficult jump in ladies' figure skating. Only America's Tonya Harding, third in the Nationals that year, was *sometimes* able to do it (Harding was another of Kwan's favorites).

Many years later, asked if she'd ever imagined winning a world title, Michelle replied: "Well, yeah. It wasn't surprising. I shot for it and I got it. . . . There was no doubt in my mind that I could do it."

Like the title character in the classic film *Rocky*, Michelle was not so much obsessed with winning as with the desire to go the distance.

At the age of ten, Michelle was to meet the person who, except for her father, would be the most important man and major influence in her young life.

Frank Carroll was a respected skating coach of the first magnitude. Around forty years old when he met Michelle, he'd had great success with Linda Fratianne, four-time U.S. champion (from 1977 through 1980), two-time world champion (1977 and 1979), and runner-up in the 1980 Olympics.

Fratianne was one of the first women to successfully perform triple jumps in competition, and Frank Carroll's expertise at teaching triples was an invaluable asset, especially in the skating world of the eighties and nineties. "To get that body in the air and make three turns, I'm afraid you've got to start them very young," said Carroll. "If you wait until they're sixteen or seventeen, it's too late."

Tiffany Chin had been Carroll's pupil. A former competitive skater himself (a medalist in three U.S. National Championships), Carroll had been coached by Maribel Vinson Owen (nine-time U.S. National champion), one of America's figure-skating legends.

Carroll's skills went beyond teaching. He understood

the intricacies of the figure-skating establishment, a world unto itself. He was a veteran at dealing with judges, choreographers, parents, the press—all (especially the media) requiring "special" attention.

He was respected by the right people, knew what had to be done in order to develop a skater, bring her along. Too many had not been properly nurtured and ended up being consumed. Timing was everything, and training a potential champion was a difficult and challenging proposition off the ice as well as on.

Coaching is a demanding profession, calling for endless hours on one's feet, in a cold-as-a-meat-locker environment, the frigid air seeping into one's bones by the end of a long, exhausting day. Whether it's figure skating or basketball, swimming or gymnastics, a coach has to know the material he's working with before he starts reaching. *You can't get it out of them unless it's in them.* . . .

Student and teacher also have to be compatible; their relationship is similar to that between a film director and an actor. The wrong chemistry will produce the wrong result. Deciding who not to teach is as important as committing to the right pupil.

The meeting of Carroll and Michelle was to prove fortuitous for all concerned.

CHAPTER THREE

❧❧

Practice Makes Perfect

Michelle always held tight to a gift her grandparents had given her as a child—a Chinese good-luck charm. A small gold rectangle, the talisman dangled from a chain around her neck; she never took it off.

It seemed she would have preferred not to take her skates off either. She loved working with Frank Carroll. Not every day on the ice was a good day, but slowly, surely he opened doors for her, taught her invaluable technique that would enable her to sustain a high level of consistency in her jumps.

Many skaters get lucky and nail a few good ones at practice or exhibitions, occasionally even in competitions—but delivering them on demand, when one is under pressure, is the name of the game. A Carroll pupil had to land a jump eight out of every ten attempts before it went into a short or long program.

Michelle took many falls—no skater, regardless of age, escapes without sore muscles, aching feet, and nasty bruise marks. "Why aren't I getting this jump? What's wrong?" is a lament heard from every skater in every rink in the course of every career. The process takes courage and persistence.

There are days when jumps you've worked so hard to achieve suddenly become impossible. What has happened? Self-discipline and perseverance are essential, and the training is indeed a metaphor for surviving in life: one has to learn to pick oneself up, brush oneself off, and move on.

"There is nothing called talent," Danny Kwan once observed. "You have to have hard work. There is one simple word: practice, practice, practice."

Michelle learned not to overtrain, not to be too anxious. One must be patient, be aware of how far to push without doing physical damage. Ruptured ligaments, resulting in "jumper's knee," could sideline a skater for weeks.

Patience is perhaps the most difficult lesson to learn—results will come in time, and the old adage is true: a journey of a thousand miles begins with the first step.

Michelle was only a kid—taking skating lessons, going to school, making friends. On the one hand, she led a totally normal life. On the other, she was obsessed with skating. She loved it; it was satisfying and great fun. There was no one yelling at her to be perfect—quite the opposite. The drive to be better came from within her.

The attention her skating brought her at the rink often coaxed a broad smile to her face. She obviously enjoyed it, and it gave her the satisfaction of knowing that she was good at something she loved to do. She was exploring her talent, her special gift.

As time went by, her mom and dad were aware that Michelle's commitment to figure skating was intensifying, not diminishing. She was fortunate to be a child who knew what she wanted to do in a world where most adults never found out!

Her parents and siblings supported her.

Within a year, a major family decision was imminent: relocating Michelle (along with her sister, Karen) to the state-of-the-art figure-skating training center at Lake Arrowhead, California. If Michelle was to pursue a competitive skating career seriously, the time had come to take this step.

Not that it would guarantee Michelle's success; on the contrary, all that was guaranteed was a total shake-up of the family's finances.

Years later, when Michelle had begun to make her mark, Danny Kwan recalled the difficulties all had faced; how his wife worked, he worked. It was hard, and Mr. Kwan was up front about not having been able to buy his daughters "fancy clothes or even good tennis shoes, okay? We struggled for a long time."

So in 1991, Michelle and her sister, Karen, were relocated to Lake Arrowhead to train. Michelle was eleven years old, Karen thirteen.

In a gorgeous setting two hours east of Los Angeles in the San Bernardino Mountains, Lake Arrowhead has long been a popular resort center, a winter wonderland in the sunny state of California. Back in the 1930s and '40s, many movie stars "escaped" to lodges there to unwind from the rigors of moviemaking.

Ice Castle Training Center is settled comfortably into more than a dozen tree-covered acres at an altitude of more than five thousand feet. The center is not merely an ice rink, it is a city within a city.

The facilities include a gym and a three-thousand-square-foot dance pavilion with a special floor designed to accommodate dance, exercise, and ballet lessons. There are courses in nutrition and sports science. There is a dormitory, a main lodge, an outdoor amphitheater, and cottages for families.

The ice rink itself, 181 feet by 85 feet, offers skaters a breathtaking view of the countryside as well as a critical view of themselves: one wall is completely mirrored. There is a cross-rink jump harness (essential for learning multirevolution jumps) and a ballet barre.

All are necessary to adequately prepare for a competitive skating career.

Twinges of homesickness did not inhibit Michelle's progress; people have remembered how Danny Kwan drove up every evening (a two-hour trip), and later "Mum" moved to Arrowhead to be with her daughters. Under Frank Carroll's tutelage, Michelle and Karen made great strides in their skating.

In Arrowhead's insular environment, Michelle's focus was sharpened as Frank Carroll worked on perfecting her technique, smoothing out any jerky movements and other bad habits. They weren't shooting for over-the-top drama in Michelle's skating at this stage. The actor Cary Grant once noted that "it takes five hundred small details to add up to one favorable impression." A champion-caliber figure skater's credo is no different.

Building up stamina and endurance is also of primary importance. A skater has to be able to appear to complete a program with the same energy as she had at the start.

* * *

One of the "secrets" of endurance is breathing; the tendency is to hold in one's breath, or to breathe minimally while concentrating intently on all that has to be done (not to mention contending with nerves).

Basic breathing was what accounted for the exceptional phrasing Frank Sinatra was capable of in his singing. Sinatra, like an athlete, had learned the "trick" of proper breathing by studying how trombonist Tommy Dorsey inhaled deeply at key moments throughout a piece, choosing spots where there was a natural "break" in the music so that the overall effect of the phrasing was continuous, seamless.

The skater's job is the same: present an uninterrupted flow of movement without huffing and puffing; never let the viewer know how hard you're working. It takes superlative technique to make any performance, singing or skating, look "effortless."

Constant repetition of a program's elements also is essential for a competitive performance. The body's muscle memory must become so accustomed to certain moves that they can be performed under extreme duress.

Michelle was taught what to do in case of a fall during a performance; she didn't think about falling, of course, but if it happened, she was to smile, keep going, and put it out of her mind—just go on to the next jump.

Plus Carroll encouraged her to tackle new moves, even if she was concerned about looking foolish. The time to fail is in the "privacy" of the training ground; one must feel free to experiment in order to find out what works and what doesn't.

Frank Carroll wanted Michelle to trust herself, her

talent, her instincts. Great performances, in any venue, were achieved when one was able to transcend fears and to work from strength.

Believe in yourself: it was a concept that would stand Michelle in great stead no matter what future endeavors awaited her.

In July 1992, she celebrated her twelfth birthday. It was the year Kristi Yamaguchi was National Senior Ladies' champion, with Nancy Kerrigan the Silver Medalist, Tonya Harding the Bronze.

Both Kerrigan and Kristi had always known the same kind of family support as Michelle. Their parents sacrificed and spent money they didn't have to foster their children's careers; it was a group effort, and each skater had the unconditional support and expertise of their coaches. Kristi had Christy Ness, and Kerrigan the Scotvolds, an estimable husband-and-wife team.

Tonya Harding, on the other hand, emerged from a reportedly dysfunctional family. The only married lady in the senior division, Harding had faced personal problems over the past three years that had adversely affected her skating career. But the sport continued to be her refuge and her hope, and the lengths to which her ambition would lead her would one day directly impinge on Michelle Kwan's career.

That year the Kwans, along with millions throughout the world, had watched on TV as Kristi Yamaguchi won Gold at the 1992 Olympics (Kerrigan placed third), then another Gold Medal a few weeks later at Worlds (Kerrigan placed second).

Both Kristi and Kerrigan had *the look*. They were beautiful young women, not "little girls," and the judges perceived "the entire package" when rating the competitors. If one didn't *look* right out there, she was behind the eight ball.

Meanwhile, Michelle won one regional competition (Southwest Pacific Junior) in 1992 and placed third in another (Pacific Coast Junior). She was slated to compete in the National Junior Championships in Orlando, Florida, and she was nervous. It was a natural reaction, and her father and coach attempted to minimize her fears by downplaying the event's importance. "It's nothing," they told her repeatedly.

However, when Danny Kwan heard Michelle talking in her sleep one night, saying over and over, "It's nothing, it's nothing," he grew anxious, and later recalled how he'd asked himself, "What am I doing to her?"

As it turned out, Michelle placed ninth in the competition. A critical heart-to-heart discussion then took place between father and daughter; Danny realized that a change in attitude toward skating was essential for both of them. "You are my daughter," he told her. "Skating has cost a lot of time and money and worry to your parents. But when I see you get too stressed out like this, I think it's time to quit." He told her he just wanted her to have fun, to enjoy skating.

She got the message.

However, Michelle had her own scenario in mind: competing at senior level at Nationals *now*, otherwise she wouldn't qualify for the '94 Olympics. She was not shy about expressing her feelings, nor was Frank Carroll reticent about overriding them.

* * *

"Little Kwan" made a decision. Carroll had said it would be best if she remained in juniors for at least another season, if not longer—he didn't want to rush her along; he'd seen too many promising talents consumed by the aftershock of a premature leap into the jaws of senior-level competition.

But quiet, obedient Michelle had her own plan, plus the determination to implement it. After all, hadn't Carroll encouraged her to have confidence in herself?

She had no intention of remaining a junior for another season. "So, when Mr. Carroll was gone," she later recalled, "I took the senior test and I passed."

When Carroll returned and learned what had happened, "he was very mad," recalled Michelle. "But he got over it."

Carroll later described his student's headstrong action as an awakening. "It scared the daylights out of her," he said. "She realized how willing she would have to become to commit herself to do more."

Things moved fast after that. Michelle won the Southwest Pacific and Pacific Coast Senior Lady titles. Then the twelve-and-a-half-year-old got her wish: she entered the 1993 Nationals as a senior lady, the youngest senior competitor in two decades.

But a "star" wasn't born overnight. Michelle placed sixth (Nancy Kerrigan won Gold, Lisa Ervin, Silver, and, once again, Tonya Harding, Bronze).

But Michelle was on her way, and reports from Nationals were that she had "electrified" the crowd. Her parents removed her from public school and engaged a private tutor to continue her education. Michelle said she didn't miss school that much, but she kind of did miss some of the kids.

Did she ever think about abandoning her schedule and just spending time with friends? She *was* with friends at Arrowhead, she said, and didn't daydream about taking a break. She wasn't feeling worn-out—just concentrating on what she had to do. Besides, skating wasn't the only pastime she enjoyed: she liked to read, write letters, swim, draw, collect things (stamps, pins, and troll dolls, which brought good luck)—just like anyone else!

Later that season, in Italy—a country she adored, especially its cuisine—Michelle won the Gardena Spring Trophy. That summer, ripples of excitement spread throughout the skating community when she finished first in the Olympic Festival in San Antonio, Texas. She was the youngest competitor ever to win the event. A record crowd of over twenty-five thousand spectators shouted their approval of her efforts.

This was a memorable moment for Michelle. "I skated great and I just felt so good!" she later said, and considered the event her most exciting experience on ice to date.

Still it wasn't all roses. She placed seventh at the Skate America event in late October. If Frank Carroll had been concerned about Michelle's future after her decision to take her senior test, his fears vanished as he saw his protégée blossom; her poise, enthusiasm, and confidence were rising to higher levels than ever.

She received *Skating* magazine's Reader's Choice Award as the figure skater of the year for 1993–1994. Many observers expressed awe at the speed with which the "newcomer" was climbing the ladder. Hearing this, Michelle offered an observation: she was hardly a newcomer—true, she was only thirteen, but she'd been skating since she was five! In her view, eight years on the ice (she was currently up to four free-skating sessions per day) was long enough for virtually anyone to make "swift" progress.

CHAPTER FOUR

～～

Building the Dream

Reflecting on her early teen years, Michelle has characterized herself as not knowing much of anything. "I never really developed my skating," she said, explaining that she had simply "jumped and jumped some more. It wasn't really artistic. I kind of smiled every once in a while. . . . But you want to feel what's inside and be able to portray it and express it to the audience."

To hear her describe her early performances, you would think she moved like a robot. But Michelle never looked like a skating windup doll. And lurking beneath the surface of her skating at this time was a ballerina eager to emerge. She just needed a little more time to develop.

Meanwhile, Michelle, thirteen going on fourteen, and the rest of the skating world became especially aware of one teenage skater, during that 1993 season, who *was* feeling what was inside and *was* able to express it to an audience.

Pay attention, young people, see what she's done. See what she's accomplished. You can do it, too! Michelle paid close attention to Oksana Baiul. Three years older than Kwan, Baiul was from the Ukraine. She'd literally burst on the scene and rocketed to the top in record time. Furthermore, she seemed to be a role model for everyone, a classic story of triumph over adversity.

Whether in competition or exhibition, spotlights or no, in a deserted rink or with spectators, Baiul could express and communicate the deep well of emotions that churned within her. Like Michelle, she was a slender adolescent, with her hair pulled back into a ponytail. Baiul was an incongruous combination of innocent child and worldly woman, a sprite mixed with a ballerina and a vaudevillian. Oksana came alive on the ice, seemed to flourish like a hothouse flower despite the bitter cold of the environment that had spawned her.

As was the case with Michelle, it wasn't necessary to prod Oksana into performing, like so many of the other girls. Rather, it was necessary to convince her to stop, to eat and sleep at least. Oksana was sensitive and had a high-strung personality. Everything and everyone aroused her curiosity and interest. Like Michelle, she was only about seven years old when she won her first competition.

Unlike Michelle, she had no father figure at home: it was strictly Oksana, her mother, and her grandparents. At the age of ten, the dark specter of death intruded on Oksana's world when one of her grandparents passed away; the following year the other died. It was terrifying for the young skater to lose them, unnerving to realize how swiftly tragedy might strike in one's life.

Then, back in August 1991, when Michelle was eleven and relocating to Lake Arrowhead to train, Oksana was approaching her fourteenth birthday and training hard for the upcoming Soviet championships. Her beloved mother suddenly took ill and was hospitalized. There seemed no reason to assume this was anything but another tough circumstance she and Mama would face together and overcome.

It was inconceivable that something bad could happen to Mrs. Baiul; she was only thirty-six years old! Unfortunately, her condition worsened rapidly; she was diagnosed with ovarian cancer, which proved terminal. Oksana was suddenly an orphan, or so it seemed. Then her coach, Stanislav Koritek, encountered her father: "He came to the funeral. He wasn't a very pleasant person, and Oksana didn't want to see him."

This crisis proved a turning point for Baiul. She felt completely alone, even with other people around her. The devastating feelings of abandonment and guilt, grief and shock, could have destroyed her.

But Oksana struggled to find and tap into the deeper something within her, so that she could continue functioning. Through her early teen years on the ice, she was, as Michelle Kwan would later become, an actress—flirtatious, sexy, and a refreshingly free spirit, radiating an infectious joy and enthusiasm for what she was doing.

Like Michelle, Kristi, and so many others, Oksana in her "prime" weighed under one hundred pounds—an asset for mastering the all-important triple jumps. The smaller and more compact one is in build, the easier and more aerodynamically feasible it becomes to properly complete multirevolutions in the air.

Skating was her beloved friend, and other skaters began to note that Oksana was an entertainer, always eager and willing to please an audience. "That's why I'm here!" she seemed to shout as her blades carried her swiftly and surely over the frozen surface.

* * *

In the sport of tennis, it is possible for a player ranked 281st to defeat the third-best player in the world; this happened on June 24, 1996, to an astounded Andre Agassi. But in skating, as Michelle Kwan was discovering, nine individuals subjectively decide the technical and artistic merits of a skater's performance. Dramatic upsets, as in other sports, simply don't occur in the skating world; the system is programmed against it.

Just as Michelle was a virtual unknown on the American scene in January 1993, so it was with Oksana Baiul that same year on the international scene when she competed in the European championships in Helsinki, Finland.

But an inner fire seemed to fuel her efforts on the evening of the long program. She smiled, flirted, projected her personality with controlled abandon. She performed a total of five triples, but none was done "in combination"—i.e., coupled with another jump (usually a double). Other competitors, on good days, performed more triples, plus the combinations, but it was the *way* Oksana performed that set her apart.

This was what Michelle and all skaters yearned to achieve—to fuse all elements into an experience for the viewer that was greater than the sum of its parts.

In a Hollywood film, the character of "Oksana" would have won the European title easily. But this was fact, not fiction, and it was the world of figure skating. She placed second.

But the ship was launched. *Who is she? What's her story?* Was the performance a fluke? Could she possibly do it again?

Overnight the newcomer had become a player of the first magnitude, but that could change without warning, as everyone knew. Inconsistency was every skater's *bête noire*.

One of the heated topics of discussion back in America was how Baiul would stack up at the Worlds against America's reigning ice princesses. Nancy Kerrigan, all agreed, had the edge. She had everything going for her—the judges were familiar with her, respected her skating style and her coaches. She had worked her way up (the judges liked that). All the elements seemed in place for that final boost up the ladder.

And what would happen at the 1993 Worlds would directly affect Michelle and her peers; it would indicate who the key players would be over the next few years. For Baiul was young enough to be a contender not only in the 1998 Olympics, but the one after that, 2002!

In Prague, on the evening of the short program at Worlds, Nancy Kerrigan's performance seemed to confirm everyone's predictions: she placed first. Oksana placed second.

For the long program, Oksana was to skate first in the final group of six (Kerrigan was next to last, a plum spot). Everyone knew the judges withheld their highest marks from those who performed early on; they had to leave "room" on their judging scale for subsequent skaters.

Baiul fell while attempting a triple-loop jump during the six-minute warm-up. The audience groaned. Kerrigan, too, had been having trouble with her jumps. On the other hand, France's Surya Bonaly, Japan's Yuka Sato, and China's Chen-Lu were doing just fine. A major upset might be looming. . . .

The warm-up over, Oksana's name was called. In a costume of royal blue and sequins, she skated confidently onto the ice, concentrating with laserlike intensity. Her coach, Galina Zmievskaia, smartly dressed and groomed, seemed more nervous than her pupil as she gave her a pep talk from the sidelines.

Oksana made the sign of the cross and took plenty of time before skating to center ice, her thoughts tightly focused. Her music began. Her face suddenly lit up as she launched spiritedly into her initial mood-establishing steps.

Throughout the program, her distinctive style combined classical ballet with pure Broadway pizzazz. She used her whole body when she skated—and most of all, her heart. A shaky landing on a double axel did little to dispel the impact of all that had come before.

Oksana playfully slapped her hands together over her head to the final beats of the music. It was over. She had performed no jump combinations (some of the other girls did do them), and had landed an imperfect double axel. . . .

Overexcited and exhausted, she fought back tears as she sat with Galina in what is known as the "kiss-and-cry area." The sophistication had vanished. She was strictly an anxious adolescent as the marks flashed on the board: 5.6s to 5.8s for content—strong, but far from unbeatable. Then the marks for artistic impression came on: 5.7s to 5.9s—very strong, but leaving ample "room" for someone to skate a better performance. Oksana burst into tears—of released tension, more than anything else—gathered up her flowers, and strode backstage, walking right by a seated Nancy Kerrigan. The two competitors ignored each other.

Kerrigan was drop-dead gorgeous in a black-and-silver Vera Wang masterpiece. The competition was hers to lose, as Nancy knew all too well (and as Michelle Kwan would one day discover). The heavy weight of everyone's expectations, including her own, was a liability that did not yet exist for Baiul.

Standing center ice waiting for her music to begin, Kerrigan seemed scared. Skating to the movie soundtrack of *Beauty and the Beast*, she missed every jump. In the kiss-and-cry area, attempts to console her were futile. "Oh my God, I just lost it. . . . I just wanna die," she cried.

Backstage, overcome by the news of her victory, Oksana once again strode by Kerrigan, neither girl acknowledging the other or exchanging a single word.

This was world competition. Interestingly, Baiul hadn't "outjumped" her rivals; France's Surya Bonaly and China's Chen-Lu ("Lulu") had completed more triples. But Baiul led the pack in artistic impression, with five of the nine judges placing her first (Kerrigan had plunged to fifth). Oksana Baiul became the youngest female skater to win a world championship since the legendary Sonja Henie (a distinction not slated to last indefinitely).

Stanislav Koritek, Oksana's former coach, was nonplussed by the extent of his onetime pupil's success. He acknowledged that she was a talented girl, "but"—and his comments would apply directly to Michelle Kwan only two years later—"everyone was surprised she did this so fast."

Michelle competed against Oksana Baiul in a Skate America event that very fall. Observing Baiul, and skating with her, was a vital moment in Michelle's development. Oksana's style was a revelation to Kwan, who immediately began to adapt elements of ballet into her own style and vowed to work hard on this aspect of her skating.

Michelle won the World Junior Championship early in 1994, exhibiting what one eyewitness has recalled as "no lack of energy or finesse. She had sparkle, grace, and stunning potential."

It was fortunate, however, that she was not the leading contender for the U.S. Senior Ladies' title that year. Nancy Kerrigan was front-runner, and Michelle's idol, Tonya Harding, was not looking forward to staring in the eyes of defeat.

In January 1994, Kerrigan was assaulted by a "mystery man" as she was training for Nationals. An incredible drama subsequently unfolded, offering the impact of a cliff-hanging TV miniseries. Woven into this incredible tale were the golden threads representing Michelle Kwan's future.

CHAPTER FIVE

You Can Do It

It was a season of high drama as Michelle's education in the world of figure skating continued to advance rapidly. She acquired an agent, an essential for any rising young talent who suddenly finds people offering her the moon. Danny Kwan chose Shep Goldberg of PMA (Proper Marketing Associates) to represent his daughter.

At the 1994 Nationals, the Kwans were astounded at the security in force at Detroit's Joe Louis Arena. At the request of Figure Skating Association personnel, in direct response to the attack on Kerrigan, police were everywhere. Who would be assaulted next? Another skater? Several skaters? An official? A group of officials?

The attack on Nancy struck a common nerve; violence was a deplorable part of today's world, and it had invaded the figure skater's domain. "Now these young athletes have one more thing to deal with as they pursue excellence in sports," observed Peggy Fleming, who fervently hoped that Kerrigan would "not let this incident destroy the bright future she's earned."

From a private box high above the arena, Nancy Kerrigan, along with her sports psychologist, her parents, her young niece, her coaches, and her agent (later husband) Jerry Solomon, could only observe the competition.

The ladies' final tonight would proceed without Kerrigan. Only time would tell if Kerrigan would be able to skate again: if the injury resulting from the attack had occurred one inch lower, it would have shattered her kneecap.

But there were other competitors in the arena with dreams to fulfill, including Michelle Kwan. "I can make it in the '94 Olympics," she said. "I'm just crossing my fingers."

While the rules declared that this year the United States could send only two ladies to the Olympics (based on the U.S. team's disappointing performance at last year's Worlds), International Competition Rule number 5.05 offered hope for a devastated Nancy Kerrigan: *The committee may also consider for [Olympic] selection other competitors who did not compete in the most recent United States Figure Skating Association Championships.*

At the conclusion of the competition, the forty-five members of the International Committee were slated to meet to determine which female skaters would qualify for the Olympic team.

The fact that Kerrigan would most likely be awarded a position on the team tightened the race even more intensely for the other competitors, Michelle included. All would be vying for the *one* remaining spot.

In the course of the Senior-level competition, the contestants skate a short and a long program. Skaters have a certain latitude in selecting elements for the short. The rules call for a mandatory double axel, but allow the skater to choose between a double or a triple jump.

The triple axel* (the only jump done from a forward outside-edge takeoff) is tops on the ladder of difficulty. In descending order, the "toe"-takeoff jumps follow—the triple lutz, triple flip, triple toe loop. Then there is the triple loop (as opposed to toe loop), which requires the skater to lift off from a back outside edge, then land on the same foot and the same edge. The triple salchow, named after its creator, Ulrich Salchow, requires a takeoff from a back inside edge.

Naturally, the more difficult the jumps performed, the more points one is awarded.

In addition, the short program requires a jump combination, chosen from the above list, plus a flying spin, a layback spin, a spin combination, a spiral sequence, and a footwork sequence.

Omitting one of the elements in the short program means a required point reduction. And attempting to repeat a failed element in the short program is forbidden.

The skater is free to choose any and all elements for the long program, which is indeed a "free" skate. No deductions are taken if an element is omitted. Nor are there deductions if one element is substituted for another mid-program. But if major elements are omitted, obviously no points for that omitted element can be awarded. However, one is permitted to repeat a failed element in the long program without being penalized.

If it sounds complicated, it really isn't; the truly difficult part is mastering all the jumps and spins and becoming consistent in performing them.

*Please see Appendix for detailed descriptions of skating jumps.

* * *

In Detroit, Michelle would be fourth to skate the short program, following Nicole Bobek, Tonya Harding, and Elaine Zayak.

There was a lesson not only for Michelle but for all skaters in the Zayak story: the importance of *attitude*. She'd been competing before Michelle was born! "I think one of the reasons I came back was to prove to myself that I could skate again," said the twenty-eight-year-old former world champion. Over the years she had lost interest in skating. "I hated the way I felt; my weight wasn't where I wanted it to be—I think it was an emotional thing. Being in the '84 Olympics, and being a star—everything just went downhill from there."

She'd considered this return to amateur skating competition very cautiously, taking a long time before reaching the decision. More confident than she'd been a decade earlier, she felt that now she was skating for *herself*.

Expectations for Nicole Bobek were high. Michelle's number-one rival, the sixteen-year-old with her shiny blond hair, blue eyes, and sexy build, was the glamour girl of the sport. At exhibitions, her repertoire included skating to Marilyn Monroe's rendition of "(We're Having a) Heat Wave." "The temperature's rising," cooed Marilyn as Nicole interpreted the bongo-drum-accented lyrics.

Audiences loved Bobek, responded to her "look." Off the ice, her private life provided a bold contrast to Michelle Kwan's. Nicole's mom was a colorful lady, and there were times when her daughter seemed to prefer partying to training. Controversy was Nicole's seemingly constant companion. She'd had a series of coaches, and was sidelined by physical injuries that kept her off the ice for weeks at a time. She could be wildly inconsistent in her skating, and the all-powerful USFSA (United States Figure Skating Association) was wary of her attitude and some alleged antics. But she had *it*, and was not to be taken for granted.

Was Michelle nervous? She loved being in front of the crowd and enjoying herself. At this point she wasn't concentrating on the pressure. She had trained herself to think that this was just a normal day and that she had to go out there and do her program as usual.

The competitors gathered for the six-minute warm-up preceding the short program, and they were a study in contrasts. Michelle was fast but careful, Harding a powerhouse, and Zayak looked nervous. Bobek was having trouble with her jumps but radiated style and energy.

Nicole took to the ice to begin her folk-dance-inspired program. She skated with flair, projecting her personality. She built up speed for the crucial triple-lutz-double-toe-loop combination, skating strong back crossovers around the rink; then, reaching back with her free leg, she tapped into the ice with her toe pick and vaulted herself into the air.

Perfect! Three revolutions, neatly landed, followed by the double toe—and no connecting steps in between.

But mistakes followed, interspersed with such memorable moments as her spiral (arabesque position) sequence, characterized by the breathtaking extension of her free leg behind her.

With Bobek, one hoped for the best—but she was erratic. Nonetheless, the judges liked her. Her marks were

relatively strong, 5.5s to 5.7. She received 5.7s and 5.8s
for artistic merit.

Tonya Harding, in red sequins, was next on the ice.
Earlier, she had noted that she could relate to Nancy Kerrigan's terrifying ordeal because she had suffered a
similar one, having received death threats before a recent
competition in Portland.

Tonya, who'd admitted with a smile that people
referred to her as "a jinx," appeared confident tonight.
Everyone acknowledged that her athletic skills were formidable, and her jumps, at their best, were unbeatable—
her sturdy legs and strong arms were capable of
propelling her high into the air and far over the ice.

The audience sat forward in their seats as Harding's
music began, and she attacked the first element in her
short program, the triple-lutz-double-toe-loop combination (the same as Bobek's). It was spectacular. Her power
was displayed again in her next move, a "death drop" sit
spin, in which she soared high into the air from a forward
outside edge takeoff, landing on the opposite foot in a
back sit spin.

Harding's spiral sequence lacked the stretch and line of
Bobek's, but she leaned so deeply into her edges and
skated with such speed that it didn't matter. The rest of
the required elements were performed with complete
control, and with a breathtaking spring to her jumps.

The judges recognized the quality of her skating. She
received a 5.7, 5.8s, and one 5.9 for technical merit. Presentation: 5.6 to 5.9.

* * *

Now the moment of truth was at hand for Elaine Zayak. Dressed in lavender and sequins, her blond hair pulled back in a ponytail, she was no longer the reed-thin child who had won the world title at age fifteen (two years older than Michelle was tonight).

It was ironic that Zayak was currently adamant in her belief that too much emphasis was being placed on jumps, for, after all, in many ways she herself had brought the change about. Indeed, she'd performed so many triples that the "Zayak rule" was devised, limiting the number of triples a skater could present in a single program.

Elaine had a lot to prove tonight. The other skaters admired her, although there had been grumbling from some quarters about permitting professionals to compete with amateurs. The crowd applauded its approval and support of Zayak's courage.

Elaine skated with conviction, taking her time and proving that she still had what it took to compete at the highest level. After the final note of music, she buried her head in her hands, relieved and happy.

The judges displayed less appreciation for Zayak's comeback. Inexplicably, one awarded her a 5.0 for content. "What did I do wrong?" she exclaimed to Peter Burroughs, her coach.

Burroughs hugged her. Elaine had placed third, behind Harding and Bobek.

Michelle was on next.

The small figure in pale blue, her long-sleeved, sequined costume glittering beneath the lights, skated onto the vast surface. She was already being referred to as "a young Kristi Yamaguchi" (Kristi was all of twenty-two years old) and being described as ambitious and competitive.

The hard-edged words didn't seem to reflect the expression on her sweet young face as she waited for her music to begin. She seemed charged with positive energy and enthusiasm.

As she began her program, elements of what would become her signature style were already in evidence: arm movements with a Far East flavor, a motif developed not only in her choreography but also on the landing of her double axel.

Michelle had devised a method of performing this treacherous required jump with a flourish that demanded great technical skill. Instead of simply riding out the landing edge while keeping her free leg in the standard position behind her, she raised the free leg higher, extended almost in a spiral position, but bent at the knee, toe pointed. No speed was relinquished on the landing while she assumed this tricky but aesthetically pleasing position, and no one else completed the jump this way.

The judges took note.

Michelle skated expressively and securely, with fluidity to her movements. Her triple-lutz-double-toe combination was neat and perfect, her spiral sequence good (and was destined to become great in the not-too-distant future). It was clear that with seasoning and maturity, she would have genuine impact as an artist.

As she completed her last steps, a broad smile lit up her face. There was nothing phony about Michelle Kwan, as a skater or a person. Over the years, her character would have a strong impact on all who watched her skate.

In this event, her technical marks ranged from 5.5 to

5.7. Artistically, despite an inexplicable 5.2, other marks ranged from 5.6 to 5.7.

Nerves were taut on the evening of the long program. Harding was in first place after the short, Bobek second, Kwan third. Zayak was close on Kwan's heels.

Michelle, wearing red, was first to skate in the final group of competitors. There was a lot on her plate this evening: six triples were planned, two in combination with doubles, plus a complex array of spins and footwork. She might be only thirteen years old, but her program would challenge any veteran.

As the music began, smoothly executed introductory moves, showcasing strong, deep edges, led to a textbook-perfect double axel, followed by one of the most difficult triples: the triple flip.

Yes!

Then a flying-camel spin, a high-torque leap from one leg to the other, landing in a back camel spin with the free leg in the arabesque position. Next, Michelle launched into a triple-lutz-double-toe-loop combination, followed by a triple-toe-loop-double-toe-loop combination.

"Amazing!" exclaimed onlookers.

At this point Michelle eased up, signaling the start of the slow section of her program. It was here that she displayed stunning artistry—the ability to deliver the goods in the "quiet" moments. It was the equivalent of a singer performing a sensitive ballad before a large audience, turning a vast auditorium into an intimate setting.

Michelle began the long lead-in edge to her triple salchow jump, leaped into the air . . . and fell. Hard. Right in front of the panel of judges.

She was up in a flash, began the preparatory steps for her

next jump, a second double axel, and landed it beautifully. Her spins displayed great promise, although in her layback spin she needed to work on deepening the arch of her back and on holding her free leg farther away from her body.

Another error: she missed her second triple lutz, landing it on two feet, but nailed the triple toe at the end. Last impressions count. A lot.

She was breathing hard but smiling broadly. It was over.

In the stands, her parents were beaming. Their daughter's technical scores ranged from 5.6 to 5.7s, artistic scores 5.6 to 5.8. A medal seemed certain.

Then again, maybe not. Elaine Zayak received a long ovation before she began. Getting back in shape had been tough, and people respected her perseverance. She proceeded to skate with authority and poise, but an aborted triple salchow (the jump Michelle had fallen on) and a fall out of her final double axel marred her efforts.

She was a strong spinner. Oddly enough, although spins, done correctly, are as difficult (sometimes more difficult) than jumps, for some reason they don't count too much in the overall picture. Many champions over the years, especially in the men's division, have had less-than-mediocre spins and it didn't seem to matter.

Zayak was nonetheless thrilled: she had proven to herself that she could do it.

Nicole Bobek, next to skate, hugged Elaine as she skated off the ice.

Glamorous in zebra-striped black-and-white sequins, Bobek was offering a program with a French music-hall motif, a stark contrast to Kwan and Zayak.

She began with great energy and speed, launching into

a high, securely landed triple lutz. When she was on, she was *on*!

However, she missed her next element, the "easiest" triple—the triple toe loop—and hit the ice with a thud. She was on her feet in an instant and launched into a powerful combination spin, then brought down the house with her spiral sequence. And so it went, more mistakes included.

Like Zayak, Bobek fell out of her final jump, a double axel. Afterward, waiting for the marks, she was in tears.

With Harding still left to skate, Michelle was, so far, in first place!

A tight, determined expression was frozen on Tonya Harding's face as she skated to center ice. It must have seemed incredible to Michelle Kwan that her idol must beat *her* to win!

Dressed in purple and sequins, her hair pulled tightly back into a ponytail, Harding launched into her program. She was skating to the dramatic soundtrack of *Jurassic Park* and her first element was a triple lutz. In height and distance, it was easily the most spectacular of the evening.

On the sidelines, Michelle Kwan's face lit up. "Wow!" she exclaimed appreciatively, watching her idol do her stuff.

Harding's second element, *if* she was going to do it, was the triple axel. Judges and spectators alike waited expectantly. She took her time with the preparation, then stepped forward into the jump—but aborted the revolutions midair, turning it into a single. The crowd groaned.

Skating with enormous power, speed, and—most important—control, Harding landed her other triples cleanly. The jumps had such "air" in them, there was a fraction of a second for her to "delay" the rotations.

Harding's program was a success, although the missed triple axel left the audience feeling disappointed.

The judges recognized the quality of her skating, awarding her 5.7 to 5.9 for technical merit, 5.6 to 5.9 for presentation.

Nancy Kerrigan gazed down at the ice from her private box as the news became official: Tonya Harding had regained the title.

Michelle won Silver, rising over the far more experienced Nicole Bobek and Elaine Zayak.

Bobek displayed a sense of humor despite her disappointing results. She later said that competing against someone like Michelle Kwan made her feel like an old lady at the ripe old age of sixteen!

Did the standings mean that Kwan, Silver Medalist, had made the Olympic team?

The Olympic Committee deliberated the question in the International Committee Room of the arena. Opinions were expressed to the effect that Kwan was still "very young," and that it was relatively easy to do what she'd done at such an early age, when everything can be done "easily." *(Easily?)*

Nancy Kerrigan had taken years to reach this point in her training and career, and for her, the opportunity wouldn't come around again. It would hardly be fair to rob her of a golden opportunity because some lunatic had attacked her!

It was decided: Kerrigan was on the team. And Tonya Harding, the new national champion—all nine judges had placed her first—had earned the right to represent the U.S.A.

"They both deserve it," Silver Medalist Michelle said, smiling. "I'm happy for them."

CHAPTER SIX

~~~

Land of the Midnight Sun

However . . . if Nancy Kerrigan or Tonya Harding had to withdraw from the Olympics for any reason, "Michelle is ready to go," said Kwan family friend Bob Clay. "She wants to be in Lillehammer. She wants to be there to skate for herself and her family."

Kerrigan seemed well on the road to recovery, although she'd lost a month of training. There were ominous signs, however, that Harding might somehow be implicated in the attack on Kerrigan.

In the meantime Michelle's coach, Frank Carroll, was mulling over important decisions regarding his pupil's future. He did not envision Michelle stylistically as a budding Tonya Harding or anyone like that. "I don't want people to say, 'There's Michelle Kwan, the girl who does the triple axel.' I want her to do a triple axel, but I want her to be known as someone who is a real artist."

Carroll was crystal clear on the type of artist he wanted Michelle to be. The greatest American skater he'd ever seen was Janet Lynn. "She had everything, the looks, the music. She was poetry. If I had my choice, that's what I'd like Michelle to be."

Who is Janet Lynn?

For five years, 1969 through 1973, petite, blond Janet Lynn was reigning U.S. champion, succeeding five-time champion Peggy Fleming, who had also won the world title three times and Olympic Gold in 1968.

Over the years there have been many figure-skating virtuosos, but Lynn's style was unique; her skating seemed a primal urge coming to life at the moment she wished to express joy. Her jumps, spins, and footwork were seamlessly integrated into a flow of movement. It was the impact of the whole, not the individual elements, that created the effect.

At age thirteen she first competed as a senior lady at Nationals; at fourteen she competed in the 1968 Olympics; at fifteen, she won her first U.S. Senior Ladies title. She was not a genius at school figures, although she deeply believed in them and had a great respect for the technique they taught her. Lynn's problems in this area prevented her from soaring to the very top in international competition, although she came close: third in the 1972 Worlds and Olympics, and second at the '73 Worlds (the year that school figures were downgraded in importance and the short free-skating program was introduced—in no small measure due to Lynn's impact on the sport).

Janet performed poorly in the short program at the '73 Worlds; she later said she felt she'd let down all the people who'd believed in her. She considered her talent a sacred gift from God, and a radiant spirituality infused her performances. She prayed fervently for better results in her long program, and skated brilliantly—but it was impossible to rise higher than second in the standings.

The camera loved Janet Lynn, and the televised championships brought her enormous popularity. She won the first World Professional Figure Skating Championship in 1973, and not only enjoyed a highly successful career as a professional, but also influenced a generation of skaters who were inspired by her artistry.

To most people it was inconceivable that anyone would turn his or her back on such material success. But the quality within Lynn that had won the admiration of so many, including Frank Carroll—who had responded to "the music" of her style, "the poetry" of her skating—had provided the motivation for her to finally step away from the arena.

She found fulfillment as a wife and mom (her five children range from age three to twenty), but has never lost her love of skating.

 ⌒⌒

Michelle shared Frank Carroll's vision of achieving the extraordinary.

On January 28, 1994, there was news that would enable Michelle to go to Lillehammer. Tonya Harding admitted that she had withheld evidence in the Kerrigan attack, and while Harding would still compete in the Olympics, Michelle now was named a team alternate.

"I don't know when we're going or where we're going," said Frank Carroll. "We're going there as an alternate unless things change. And then she [Michelle] will be put on the ice."

The changes Carroll referred to concerned Harding's near future and whether or not the police would be able to produce evidence to implicate her in the crime. Michelle said she was trying not to think about Harding's situation. "I just skate," she said.

She'd never been to "the Land of the Midnight Sun," a name that refers to the fact that from May to July, the sun shines in Norway at night as well as the day, but Michelle, like all figure skaters, was familiar with the country for a special reason. "Sonja Henie is who we all want to be," explained Dorothy Hamill.

A skater could no more ignore the legend of Norway's Sonja Henie than a student of politics could be oblivious to John F. Kennedy or Franklin D. Roosevelt.

∽∼

Who was Sonja Henie?

As a child, when she heard music, she wanted to express in motion the way it made her feel.

Sonja Henie's life on ice, like Michelle Kwan's, began when she was barely more than a toddler. "I was fortunate," she recalled. "I discovered what I loved to do and wanted to do from a very early age."

As with Michelle, from the beginning Sonja had a solid support system: her family, including an older brother, Leif. Her parents, Wilhelm and Selma, were willing to underwrite their daughter's heart's desire, and the Henies had an added advantage to assist in her dream: wealth.

At the age of six, after months of pleading with her mom and dad, Sonja received her first pair of skates. At seven, competing against skaters twice her age, she won her first competition. By the age of twelve she was champion of Norway and entered her first Olympics (the 1924 Games). She placed last.

That was one of the last times Sonja Henie was not the leader of the pack. In 1927, at age fifteen, she became the youngest female ever to win a world championship (a record that remained unchallenged for seventy years).

Sonja's other great passion was ballet, and she was the first in amateur competition to boldly combine dance and figure skating, an innovation that was swiftly recognized as brilliant. In retrospect, she viewed her contribution as a mixed blessing: "It is a great deal easier to beat opponents who lack your weapons than to beat them sheerly by your skill in using weapons."

She also fearlessly changed the way female skaters in amateur competition looked: shorter, less cumbersome skirts, and beige-colored, then white boots (both already accepted in the ranks of professionals) all became standard equipment.

The petite, blue-eyed blond eventually set her sights on a Hollywood career, a distinction no other figure skater had achieved. "I want to do for figure skating what Fred Astaire has done for dancing," she said.

"Impossible," she was told emphatically. "No

figure skater can 'carry' a picture. It's never been done. You can be a featured act, but established stars must carry the film."

During this time Sonja learned a universal lesson: *ignore negative advice when you are certain of what you are doing.* Sonja's father was her rock, guiding her when she might have faltered. "I've signed Miss Henie and her skates," noted mogul Darryl F. Zanuck. "Even if she couldn't skate, I'd have signed her anyway, but not for so much money."

During Hollywood's golden era, Sonja rocketed to the very top as a box-office attraction. During her peak years, only Clark Gable and Shirley Temple were bigger draws.

Sonja's greatest regret was that her father didn't live to see her succeed in films. But he was beside her all through her "amateur" career: to the present day, no singles skater has equaled (or come close to equaling) Sonja's competitive record: *three* consecutive Olympic Gold Medals, *ten* consecutive World Championships.

It should be both inspiring and comforting for today's skaters to learn that Sonja was able to keep her career as a professional in high gear for two decades! She was a visionary: Henie coproduced and starred in her own touring ice show, which attracted huge crowds year after year. She wasn't the first in the history of figure skating to do this, but like Elvis Presley in the world of rock music, she carried her chosen field to undreamed-of heights, jolting the public into an awareness of skating that hadn't existed before.

She never lost her competitive spirit. When she was thirty-six years old, she wanted to launch an annual World Professional Figure Skating Championship, and challenged the new nineteen-year-old Olympic champion, Canada's Barbara Ann Scott, to a skate-off! It was a concept twenty-five years ahead of its time.

Sonja was more than a skater—she was an experience. Who could forget the sight of the diminutive champion, at the age of forty-four, with her mom in tow, breaking in a new pair of boots at the old Iceland rink in midtown Manhattan? And on that occasion, Mama Henie, obviously following a ritual that began when Sonja was six, proceeded to lace up her daughter's skates!

After a decade in retirement, in the late 1960s Sonja reactivated her skating career (just at the time Janet Lynn was emerging as *the* prominent young talent on the skating scene). Henie produced and starred in a new skating film, *Hello, London.* ("She was wonderful in it," recalled skating legend John Curry.)

Stricken suddenly with leukemia, Sonja died in 1969, only fifty-seven years old. Sonja's ultimate goal had been to become a true artist of the ice. Her definition of an artist? "The ability to give you something you had not been able to imagine in advance."

Thanks to Sonja Henie, ice skating became (and has remained) one of the most popular sports throughout the world.

As the 1994 Olympic Games progressed, Tonya Harding's reputation unraveled at an alarmingly rapid rate. The entire skating community heard the developing story about the FBI investigation of the "Tonya business." Exclamations of "Oh, wow!" now applied to the latest revelations in the case, and Michelle, and much of the rest of the world, looked on as Tonya's effort to skate to glory came screeching to a halt!

Michelle would have plenty to tell her grandchildren about. As an alternate and not a team member, she practiced daily in the city of Oslo, which was two hours away from Hamar, scene of the competition. Because she wasn't a team member, she was not permitted to take part in the opening ceremonies or even to visit the Olympic village. She later said that it hadn't felt like "an Olympic experience."

But she was kept informed. Oksana Baiul had endured her own experience with violence at the Games. It occurred during practice, the day before the long program. Skaters always zoomed around the rink (twenty miles per hour was average top speed), weaving swiftly in and out of each other's paths (common procedure on practice ice; Michelle did it every day).

All knew each other's preparatory steps for jumps and spins; out of the corners of their eyes one always looked out for danger, prepared to skid to a halt at an instant's notice.

Oksana and Germany's Tanja Szewczenko didn't see each other coming until the sickening thud of their colliding bodies reverberated through the rink. Shock gave way to horror as everyone realized what had occurred.

Oksana had had the wind knocked out of her. As she

was helped from the ice, she looked like an injured bird. There was a gash in her shin, and her back had been wrenched. Szewczenko had bruised her hip and abdomen. Doubt was expressed whether either girl would be able to perform, especially Baiul, from whose wound blood was dripping.

As far as Oksana was concerned, once she'd recovered from the shock, there wasn't the slightest question of whether or not she'd skate.

Her wound required stitches. The doctors explained that the pain she would feel could be deadened with shots of a drug approved by the Olympic Committee. Oksana was urged to withdraw; she didn't want to end up disabled, did she? It was a real possibility.

The next evening, Michelle was in the stands as Baiul and Kerrigan stood shoulder to shoulder on the sidelines, not exchanging a word, both observing a crimson-clad Harding perform her long program.

Perhaps the most bizarre and at the same time saddest moment occurred when Harding, after missing the first element of her long program, the triple lutz, skated over to the referee and, fraught with emotion, hiked her foot up on the barrier and displayed a torn shoelace.

The tearful Harding was permitted to correct the situation, forcing the next skater, France's Josée Chouinard, to step in to perform earlier than anticipated. Chouinard's concentration dissolved, and her performance suffered badly.

Tonya subsequently skated her program, but with not much better results.

Still the competition was far from over. Skating

back-to-back, Nancy Kerrigan would perform before Oksana Baiul.

Nancy delivered a stunning, almost mistake-free performance. Oksana, able to hear the thunderous applause for her rival's efforts, skated onto the ice, gathering her thoughts and her strength as the computer tabulated Nancy's scores. Victory was Kerrigan's, or so it seemed.

Oksana never expected anything to be easy. She viewed this challenge as another life lesson, another "test," and reached deep within herself to tap the spiritual well that fed her soul.

The injections she had received had deadened the pain, but she retained all feeling in her body. She realized she mustn't make any mistakes, and went on to boldly articulate each move, attack each jump. However, like Kerrigan, she made a mistake, landing a triple flip on two feet. A blink of the eye and one missed the error; it was unlikely, however, that all nine judges had blinked at the same instant.

Then, later, another mistake: she doubled a toe loop intended as a triple.

Then the adrenaline kicked in. Lesson: one could think clearly out there as long as the focus was on what *had* to be done rather than on what one *hadn't* done. Oksana made an instantaneous decision: *add some jumps*. She had to, or she'd lose.

She inserted a triple toe loop to make up for the one she'd missed, and at the end of the program—*very* risky, because she was tired and had slowed down—a double axel in combination with a double toe loop. Imperfect, but daring and gutsy.

Michelle took note.

The final note of music! It took a moment for Oksana's

mind to catch up to what her body had accomplished. She put her hands up to her head, to keep it from splitting! Involuntary sobs of relief burst forth as she collapsed breathlessly in her coach's arms.

An ordinary person had been forced to meet an extraordinary challenge; she'd triumphed in the face of adversity. It had been a breathtaking and inspiring display of courage.

The moment wasn't lost on Michelle Kwan.

It took some moments for Oksana to regain control over her emotions. She was the same fifteen-year-old she'd been four minutes earlier. To the world, however, a metamorphosis had occurred. She'd entered the rarefied atmosphere inhabited by superstars. And she took home the gold.

It was a lesson in survival on the ice that Michelle Kwan was not likely to forget: *it was possible for one to think very fast on one's feet—literally.*

Kerrigan won Silver, missing out on first place by one-tenth of one point in artistic impression from one judge (the East German). Tonya Harding placed tenth.

CHAPTER SEVEN

~~~

Land of the Rising Sun

A surprise was in store for Michelle Kwan: neither Oksana Baiul, Nancy Kerrigan, nor Tonya Harding would compete at the World Championships the following month. Baiul and Kerrigan were turning professional, Harding had been banned from competition by the USFSA as a result of the Kerrigan attack, and therefore Michelle, now the top-ranked American skater, *would* be permitted to compete. She'd be the youngest woman ever to represent the U.S.A. in world competition.

The media was ready and waiting for Michelle in Chiba, Japan, when she arrived for the event in March. She seemed to take the attention in stride; yes, she realized that if it had been an "ordinary" competitive year, she might not be here at all. But there had been nothing ordinary about this year.

According to the rules, Michelle's tiny shoulders would bear the responsibility of ensuring that at least two U.S. female skaters would go to Worlds next year. To accomplish that, she'd have to place in the top ten.

Did that place undue pressure on a thirteen-year-old?

It was true that any opportunity to gain valuable experience *out* of the spotlight had been forfeited, but Kwan was not an isolated soul in Japan. In addition to the rest of the U.S. skating team—and Michelle was flattered to be one of them—her parents and sister, Karen, were on hand, along with coach Frank Carroll and Irina Rodnina, former ten-time world and three-time Olympic pair champion from Russia. Now headquartered back in the U.S. at Lake Arrowhead, Rodnina was for the moment working with Carroll on coaching Michelle.

Rodnina harbored no illusions about the denizens of the competitive skating world. "We have a saying in Russia," she said. "Each soldier desires to be a general. If you don't want to work to be a general, why are you here?"

An old Japanese legend tells how the goddess of the sun sent one of her sons to rule the islands of Japan. While many Japanese call their country "Nippon," which means "source of the sun," Westerners often call Japan "the Land of the Rising Sun."

It was Michelle's first visit to the country, and she looked forward to revisiting on a more leisurely schedule, since the 1998 Winter Olympics were to be held in the city of Nagano.

How did Michelle feel, going to her first Worlds? "I remember walking into the arena, seeing all the top skaters," she recalled. Then it hit her: *This is Worlds, oh my God!* I'm competing against *them*?"

Michelle would shortly be competing against other formidable skaters who'd competed in Lillehammer.

Bronze Medalist Chen-Lu was a genuine threat; her lyrical style enchanted viewers. She appeared feather-light on her feet but was deceptively powerful, able to deliver even the most difficult triples with elegance, style, and grace.

And there was the dynamic French and European champion Surya Bonaly, a powerhouse jumper whose peculiarly gymnastic style was highly respected by the judges (and rewarded accordingly).

Michelle was beside herself when one day she found herself sitting next to Midori Ito. "I was in awe," she recalled. "It was like I wasn't even there. I was molecule floating."

What was Michelle's goal here? She simply "wanted to do the best I could ever do." She'd practiced the elements in her short and long programs thousands of times. She'd performed the programs so often that she could (and undoubtedly often did) do them in her sleep, visualizing positive results.

But it was her first Worlds, and she later acknowledged that it had been tough. The night before the short program, Michelle had a long conversation with herself. "You have to do it," she kept repeating. "Come on, you can do it!"

With the cheers of her teammates ringing in her ears, Kwan presented a short program that landed her in eleventh place. For a first-time showing, with the international judges unfamiliar with her persona and style, and considering that she missed a triple lutz, things went better than might have been expected.

Despite her lapse, two triple lutzes were planned for the long program—a program which would count for two-thirds of the score.

* * *

A couple of days later, as Danny, Estella, and Karen Kwan sat nervously in the stands, Michelle, costumed in red, skated to center ice for the long program. There was no American judge on the panel, so "Little Michelle Kwan," all four feet nine inches and ninety-seven pounds of her, was out there on her own in more than one sense of the term.

She smiled—"I only did it because another skater bet me five dollars I couldn't," she later joked—and sailed into a routine packed with the most difficult items on the skating menu.

The crowd loved her; she had that something extra. Her double axel was perfect. A strong triple-lutz-double-toe combination, however, was marred by a step in between, and she had to touch her hand down on the ice to keep from falling on a triple toe loop. But the slow section of her program was lyrical, and a second, very solid triple lutz was sensational. All elements had been blended into a fluid, well-thought-out pattern of choreography.

People were on their feet applauding, including, of course, the Kwans. Danny "high-fived" everyone in his vicinity. Michelle acknowledged the ovation and skated over to kiss-and-cry, clutching a number of stuffed animals and flowers, gifts from fans.

Wearing a cowboy hat a fan had tossed out to her, she smiled stoically when the audience groaned as her marks were shown on the board. A low 5.0 up to a respectable 5.6 flashed up for her technical marks. An absurdly low 4.8, ranging up to a 5.5 (from the Chinese judge), acknowledged her artistic performance.

The often inscrutable world of figure-skating judging had reared its ugly collective head. What mattered, one had to remember, was not how high or low the individual scores were, but where each judge had placed her. A 5.6 could mean a first place from one judge, if he'd rated all other competitors lower. The skater with the most first places won; the skater rated second by a majority of the judges placed second, and so on.

Michelle had wanted to do "the best I could," and despite some overly critical judges, she had. She'd moved up to eighth place—and thereby ensured that two female U.S. skaters would go to the Worlds next year.

Once again, Kwan was witness to a competitor's unexpected and not very admirable behavior. A teary-eyed Surya Bonaly was so disappointed on winning Silver (Chen-Lu had been awarded Gold) that at first she adamantly refused to permit the official to place the medal around her neck!

This created a minor scandal—unfortunate, because Bonaly was otherwise a polite and charming person—and was definitely a lesson in how not to conduct oneself.

Kwan's abilities, along with Nicole Bobek's, were tested later in the season against those of professional skaters, including Caryn Kadavy and Rosalynn Sumners. Intrigued by the prospect of competing against "pros" for the first time, Michelle was starstruck. She was meeting skaters she had grown up watching on TV. "Can I have your autograph?" she asked Paul Wylie.

Caryn Kadavy, Bronze Medal winner in the 1987 Worlds, was fascinated by Michelle. "I worry for kids who have all the jumps so young," she said, "because what happens if they grow and spurt?" Kadavy was twenty-six, and spoke from experience. Physical changes could precipitate disaster, "unless [Michelle] doesn't change that much, like Kristi Yamaguchi. She was like Michelle Kwan, and she just stayed the way she was."

Kwan was already inches taller than she'd been at the beginning of the 1993–1994 season. Frank Carroll had detected a change in the timing of her jumps. He recognized the necessity of allowing her body the proper rest to develop properly. As far as he was concerned, his job was to keep Michelle interested in skating throughout the inevitable vicissitudes of her career.

At the Hershey's Kisses U.S. Pro-Am Championships, there was prize money at stake ($40,000 to the Gold Medal winner).

Michelle's growing reputation was not based on perfection, and she wasn't perfect on this occasion. But the idea was not to permit a mistake to throw her into confusion. Developing one's concentration is perhaps the most difficult challenge of all; cultivating the ability to release fears and control emotions is more arduous than any jump or spin.

At one point in her program, she stumbled when simply skating forward ("I tripped on my foot," she said, "I was kind of nervous before the triple lutz"), but recovered instantly and forged on.

The judges rewarded her expertise with 5.8s and 5.9s for technical ability, 5.6 to 5.8s for artistic merit.

"Little Michelle" won $30,000, placing second to Caryn Kadavy. More important, the event added to the prestige and respect she was gaining. Michelle's view on competing against the pros? "It was fun," she said.

Then she went on to win Gold at the esteemed International Figure Skating Challenge later in the season.

CHAPTER EIGHT

❦

Moving Closer

"It would be great to be the next national champion," mused Michelle. "I don't think there's any pressure, though. I'm still the underdog."

And she was still the quintessential young teenager, an image that was both an asset and a liability. An asset because it's who she really was, at age fourteen; a liability because it wasn't "the look" that went hand in hand with a Gold Medal in the Senior Ladies division, neither here nor abroad.

She'd proven her mental and physical stamina, and was working hard on improving her line and extension and on refining and defining her style. And she was working on the triple axel, which "isn't quite there yet."

Choosing the proper music for a program is a vital decision, underestimated by most nonskaters and even by skaters. Music must support and enhance the visual picture, not overwhelm it with a wall of sound. It is incredible how many skaters and their coaches choose inappropriately, and more incredible yet how many skaters haven't the faintest idea of how to interpret the music. Thrusting out an arm or leg to coincide with an accent in the score does not constitute "interpretation."

Michelle possessed this interpretive talent, an ability to live within the music, to express with movement what the composer was communicating through his melodies.

For her long program at this year's upcoming Nationals, Michelle's music was an ideal selection: Saint-Saens's "Rondo Capriccioso," dramatic but at the same time light and airy, a perfect complement to Michelle's style.

Kwan was a favorite going into the 1995 Nationals; her work ethic, her consistency, her coaching team, and her personality had won her many admirers. She was a spokesperson for the Children's Miracle Network and made a practice of donating all the stuffed animals fans gave her to the Los Angeles Pediatric Hospital. At Christmastime, she put on a Santa Claus hat and brought the animals to the hospital, spending time with the youngsters. Michelle's motto seemed to be, "If you are a friend, you'll have friends."

Nicole Bobek, now seventeen, had made a major change in her support team: she'd been working with a new coach, Richard Callaghan. Nicole's talent was never in question, but devising an approach to consistent mental preparedness had proven an elusive task. Mrs. Bobek found herself impressed with Michelle Kwan's progress, and with her ability to remain focused on the goal and not become bored.

The dark horse in the championship was twenty-four-year-old Tonia Kwiatkowski. If she became national champion, she'd be the "oldest" woman to win since Maribel Vinson (who later coached the young skater Frank Carroll) in 1937. This was no less than Kwiatkowski's ninth attempt at capturing the title! She was highly respected by the "official" skating community, for her choice of coach (Carol Heiss Jenkins), her lifestyle (she was currently a college student), and her perseverance.

Last year, when thirteen-year-old Michelle had burst on the scene, she'd hurtled past Tonia to win the third spot on the Olympic team. Tonia had just earned her bachelor's degree from Baldwin-Wallace College in Berea, Ohio, with a double major in psychology and communications.

Michelle wasn't even born when Tonia, almost nine years old, began taking skating lessons. "I remember this tiny body with great rotation," recalled her coach, Carol Heiss. "Tonia was one of the better ones, and she worked very hard. After about three weeks, her mother came over and asked me to work with her."

The emphasis was the same as it had been with Michelle. "When you're young, you jump, jump, jump, spin-spin-spin. But now I go back and look at my tapes and I see it wasn't natural," recalled Tonia.

She had placed third in the '93 Nationals. In '94, when Michelle was runner-up, she finished fifth. She dealt with the blow by returning to college. "I told myself, 'Get a job, use your major.' " After two weeks, however, she was bored. "I saw my friends sitting around watching the soaps." She ventured back on the ice. "One day I walked in with my skating clothes. I told my coaches, 'I feel like skating,' and I kept going back."

And she was here, at the 1995 Nationals being held in Providence, Rhode Island. Of all the entrants in the Senior Ladies' category, only the Gold and Silver Medalists would qualify for the world team this year. Tonia

Kwiatkowski longed to be among them. What a birthday present that would be—the next day she was turning twenty-four.

Karen Kwan was competing this year in the same division as Michelle; they were the first sisters to compete together in Senior Nationals since 1959. If a rivalry existed between them, it was not discernible. Neither took her familial relationship for granted, nor would either risk endangering it. It was obvious the girls loved and respected each other.

Karen's style of skating was quite different from Michelle's. Several inches taller, Karen was elegant and ethereal, and shared her sister's ability to interpret music. While her spins were lovely, to date her repertoire of jumps lacked a couple of the requisite triples.

"Fortune is not on the side of the fainthearted," said Sophocles, and Michelle didn't lose heart when she skated a flawed short program in the 1995 Nationals. To many people's surprise and dismay she finished third, behind Tonia Kwiatkowski and Nicole Bobek.

On the evening of the long program, Kwiatkowski, Bobek, and Kwan were the final three competitors to skate.

Tonia's face was a study in steely determination as she assumed her opening stance, waiting for her music to begin. She performed aggressively, making only one major error: she fell on a triple flip, one of the most difficult triples, but recovered so swiftly that the overall effect wasn't spoiled.

Tonia's parents, Shirley and Leonard, just like Michelle's,

were in the audience watching her. The couple was thrilled; their daughter's scores were strong.

Unofficially, Kwiatkowski was the leader so far.

Then Nicole Bobek skated onto the ice. She looked stunning, her blond hair braided into a twist at the back of her head, fastened with a jeweled clip. She wore a gleaming blue, open-back costume trimmed with sequins, created by Kristi Yamaguchi's designer.

Skating to the soundtrack of *Dr. Zhivago*, she was off like a rocket. She built up enormous speed, preparing for her first jump, the triple lutz. She rode out the long, back outside preparatory edge, reached back with her free leg, tapped into the ice with her toe pick, and vaulted herself high into the air.

Yes!

She was skating confidently, her movements smooth and fluid. Next came the triple flip, the jump Kwiatkowski had fallen on. Once again, Nicole built up high speed, took her time with the sweeping forward preparatory edge-and-three turn leading into the toe-pick takeoff of the jump, and landed another big one, tacking on a double toe loop for good measure.

However, attempting the "easiest" of the triples, a triple toe, she almost fell, just managing to keep herself upright on the landing.

After a first-rate double axel, an element she'd missed in the short program, it was obvious that the erratic "blond bombshell" was having one of her better nights.

Her magnificent spiral was the highlight of the last section of her program; a salchow intended as a triple turned into a double, but there would be no deductions. All skaters were free to change and substitute elements in the long program; Nicole simply wouldn't get credit for doing the triple.

She hit a bull's-eye with a second triple toe, completing a technically powerful program that was a surprise to everyone. Her new coach, Richard Callaghan, was delighted. The judges were, too: technical marks ranged from 5.6 to 5.9, presentation marks were 5.7 to 5.9s, and Bobek moved into the lead as Tonia Kwiatkowski, on the sidelines, sipped from her bottle of mineral water and smiled weakly.

Michelle, clean-cut in pink and a ponytail, had her work cut out for her. Frank Carroll gave her a few final words of encouragement and advice (he'd expressed concern after the warm-up that she'd done too much and may have left her best work on the practice ice).

But Michelle had read a prophetic message in a fortune cookie: *you're entering a time of great promise*. More significantly, an inner radiance and growing maturity were evident in her demeanor.

"Ladies and gentlemen, representing the Los Angeles Figure Skating Club, please welcome Michelle Kwan!"

An ovation greeted her appearance. People *liked* her. Smiling, she confidently began her opening choreography, which led directly into a superb double axel, complete with the unique Kwan landing.

The poignant violin figure in her music seemed to deepen the intensity of her efforts. She launched into a triple flip, followed by a spin sequence. Then strong back crossovers around the rink led into the treacherous triple lutz—the element she'd missed in the short program.

On target! Preparing to step into a triple toe loop, however, she somehow skidded over the entrance to the jump, but without missing another step, she simply repeated the entrance and landed the jump cleanly. Watching Oksana and all the others had paid off. In an emergency, one had to think fast!

Michelle looked the judges in the eye as she skated past them, preparing for a triple salchow; she landed it with grace and confidence. But her next jump was a failure: she stopped dead on the landing of her triple loop. Ignoring the gaffe, she went on to her next element, a beautiful glide diagonally across the rink (the move, the Ina Bauer, was named for its creator, the late German pairs skater).

It was evident throughout her performance that Michelle had made great progress in developing a more mature style. Her swift, light footwork paved the way for a second triple lutz, but her speed entering the jump was too slow, and she fell on the landing.

As she'd been taught, she was up in a flash, forcing a broad smile—just as she'd practiced it, in case of such an emergency—and delivered a textbook-perfect triple toe. A final blur spin and the program was over.

Michelle appeared happy.

An unsmiling Danny Kwan, wearing jeans and a wind-breaker, couldn't remain in his seat. He climbed over his wife and daughter and stood in the aisle, looking down at the arena below as Michelle, in kiss-and-cry, clutched a teddy bear and flowers.

Her scores seemed interchangeable with Bobek's: 5.6 up to 5.9 technically, 5.6 to 5.9 artistically. The leaders had all made errors, but all had skated well.

Alone backstage, having exchanged her *Zhivago* costume for a white shirt, slacks, and sneakers, Nicole

Bobek looked younger than her seventeen years. She sat alone, unaware for a few seconds more that she'd won the title.

She greeted the news with elation and disbelief.

Michelle had placed second. "I'm fine," she said. "I don't look back. There's no more or no less pressure on me than if I had won. You don't get pressure from anyone else, you get it from inside yourself."

Tonia Kwiatkowski placed third, Karen Kwan seventh. Bobek and Michelle would be going to Worlds.

The hard work, the pain and suffering, as Nicole described it—all had paid off.

Michelle's feelings? She denied that expectations for her to win had gotten the best of her. She'd wanted to skate well and, except for the fall, felt she had. The pressure hadn't gotten to her for three good reasons: she had a wonderful family, a wonderful coach, and everything was going well.

The route all envisioned for Michelle would require careful navigation. "One of the big issues we face today is that Michelle is only fourteen years old," observed her agent, Shep Goldberg. "Michelle should be around a long, long time. This is a marathon, not a hundred-yard dash."

CHAPTER NINE

"Plenty of Time Ahead of Her . . ."

Michelle spent little, if any, time contemplating the vagaries and intricacies of figure-skating judging or worrying how she was perceived as a contender for the title.

Such matters were the province of her father, her coach, and her agent, none of whom was pleased at how the judges had rated Michelle at Nationals.

Her skills were fine-tuned even further in ensuing weeks before the Worlds. While she was skating the same short and long programs, the placement of the elements was juggled a bit. The triple-lutz-double-toe-loop combination, usually performed well into the short, was now her opening salvo, and a triple flip had been substituted for the less difficult triple toe.

By increasing the difficulty factor, one assumed the technical scores would increase accordingly.

About a hundred miles northwest of London, England, and about seventy-five miles southeast of Liverpool, birthplace of The Beatles, lies the city of Birmingham. The region around Birmingham was once called "the black country" because the city's many roaring factories poured forth so much sooty smoke.

Birmingham was the site of the 1995 World Championships, and Michelle had high hopes for her chances in the event. She never doubted that delivering the goods on the ice would result in appropriate acknowledgment by the judges.

As competitors descended on the city from all over the world, it was obvious that this would be "a real horse race."

There was considerable controversy surrounding Nicole Bobek. She'd had a "wild child" tag planted on her by the media; what might be described as her youthful sense of adventure had recently resulted in an incident that was magnified into major tabloid headlines, especially in Britain.

Bobek and her mom dealt with the unwanted attention as best they could. The fact that Nicole had changed coaches frequently fueled the fire of her "prima donna" image. When she was Michelle's age, Bobek recalled she'd been jealous when she saw other fourteen-year-olds laughing and having a good time. She wanted a "normal" life, like theirs, but would have to stop skating to achieve it. She'd had to ask herself, did she want a normal life? Her answer had been no.

And here she was, in Birmingham, seeking the world title, competing against countryman Kwan. Michelle, at this point in her life, had been skating three hours a day, seven days a week, training with weights, taking dance lessons, paying special attention to diet, and absorbing two and a half hours of daily tutoring.

* * *

The warm-up sessions were fascinating as eyes focused on Kwan, Bobek, Bonaly, Chen-Lu (who was recovering from a stress fracture in her foot and was experiencing stomach problems), and myriad others. The sound of the skaters' blades "damaging" the ice echoed through the arena as competitors and their coaches sized each other up, accustomed themselves to the surroundings, ran through their programs, practiced their jumps and spins.

Predictably, the media flocked around Bobek, who had no comment about anything. There was no question that she had the momentary edge; she was American champion and looked the part.

Michelle, her face scrubbed clean, hair in a ponytail, sometimes looked even younger than her fourteen and a half years. But she was aglow. She appeared to derive great satisfaction from being a member of the team, of having moved closer to her goal.

The road to figure-skating gold, however, has usually been a circuitous one. Although Michelle wasn't aware of it, she did not have the inside track. Not that it was impossible for her, or someone like her, to cause an upset and win. It was also possible to invent a jump that called for five revolutions in the air, but it wasn't likely.

Maintaining a positive attitude was an essential element in preserving Michelle's enthusiasm and outlook. She went along on a brief sightseeing trip to historic London, another first in her world travels. But when it came time for the business at hand, Michelle once again proved she deserved the great faith in her potential and her abilities so many people had shown.

Dressed in a blue, gray, and white costume that resembled a watercolor sprinkled with sequins, she offered the required elements in a short program that showcased her intricate footwork, her ever-more-elegant spirals, and her perfectly centered spins.

The program was a winner, and the audience acknowledged it. Her father, seated in the stands, was thrilled. He stood up excitedly and blew her a kiss. Her mom's smile was a mile wide.

A radiant smile on Michelle's face was accompanied by a forceful thumbs-up sign as she skated over to kiss-and-cry, where Frank Carroll greeted her with a kiss on the cheek.

Inexplicably—yet somehow predictably to those familiar with the system—although she'd skated virtually a technically perfect short program, the international judges were unnecessarily conservative: 5.4 to 5.8s for required elements, 5.5 to 5.9 (from one judge) for presentation. They awarded higher technical marks to others, including Surya Bonaly, whose mistake-heavy presentation was apparent even to a nonskater! Bonaly had skated directly after Kwan, so the contrast between the two was blatant.

Although Chen-Lu skated at a faster pace than Michelle, she'd let her free leg swing wide and was barely able to save her triple-lutz-double-toe combination. She was wobbly on spins, and other elements were not completed as neatly and precisely as Kwan's.

It didn't seem to matter.

Frank Carroll, Danny Kwan, and the rest of Michelle's support team realized what was going on. Apparently, the Kwan persona was simply "too young." "The other girls, I thought, looked older," Carroll later observed. There was no way the judges were going to bestow medal-caliber scores, even though deserved, on "a kid who's got plenty of time ahead of her."

Carroll and company would do their best to protect Michelle's ego from undue damage. She was a trouper and eager to deliver the long program she'd been perfecting so diligently.

Nicole Bobek, striking in white and sequins, appeared apprehensive backstage, awaiting her chance to skate in the short. "Relax," her coach told her. Once she got out on the ice, she was exciting and charismatic, and skated with confidence and strength (although without doing a triple flip, which Michelle performed consistently).

Bobek had a physical sophistication that set her apart from the crowd. "Awesome," declared her coach afterward as she skated to kiss-and-cry.

Bobek won the short, followed by Russia's Olga Markova, Chen-Lu, and Surya Bonaly.

Michelle was in fifth place.

Kwan would be last to skate the long program; she'd have to cool her heels throughout most of the evening. "I didn't want to watch the other skaters," she later said. "I knew it would make me nervous."

The arena was packed, the air charged with excitement and anticipation. Many were angry that Michelle had been "robbed," while others were rooting for Bobek and for longtime European favorite Surya Bonaly.

Now twenty-one years old, Bonaly had built up quite a following over the years. Like Scott Hamilton, she performed a terrific back somersault—illegal in Olympic-division competitions—landing hers on one foot! She had stopped the show on many occasions when skating in exhibitions. But first to skate in the long program was Nicole Bobek.

Skating to *Dr. Zhivago*, Bobek's opening moves in the long program surpassed her spectacular efforts at the U.S. Nationals.

"Work hard, be proud of yourself," Bobek's coach had advised her. And after a powerhouse triple-lutz-triple-toe-loop combination, there seemed little doubt that the world crown would be hers.

Mid-program, however, Bobek's concentration, along with her stamina, faltered; the spell was broken, and she fell hard on a triple-loop jump. Moments later she took another spill, attempting a triple salchow.

Perhaps she'd begun thinking too much out there. Now she'd have to fight to win any medal at all. She managed a strong double axel, and skated a respectable finale.

Tears stung her eyes as she skated over to kiss-and-cry. Barely able to maintain her composure, her face was a portrait of frustration and disappointment as she gazed up unhappily at the screen: 5.5 to 5.8 for required elements, 5.4 to 5.9 for presentation. Not that bad, considering. She managed a weak smile.

Chen-Lu, her dark hair pulled tight into a chignon, lips rouged crimson red, looked striking in a crimson costume; square-cut neckline in front, plunging V-neckline in back, and not a sequin to be seen; it was a perfect complement to her beauty.

"I want to combine my Asian heritage with a sport that originated in the West," she'd said when describing the theme of her long program.

Over the past four years the judges had seen her blossom from the fourteen-year-old who'd entered her first Worlds and placed twelfth. She'd grown inches and put on pounds and was encountering the usual skater's problems adapting her jumps and spins to her "new" eighteen-year-old body.

The combination of her looks, her music (Far East and classical European), and her choreography proved memorable. The concept had been devised by Toller Cranston, whose daringly original skating style had revolutionized the sport back in the 1970s. With Chen-Lu, Cranston had deliberately avoided any glitz or California-style glamour. He strove for a total impression; in his view, that was why Kristi Yamaguchi had enjoyed such success.

Chen-Lu's long program delivered a solid series of triple jumps interspersed with intricate footwork and spins. There was a strong structure to her program, an exciting tension fusing all the elements.

The judges appreciated her efforts: 5.6 to 5.8s for technical merit, 5.8s and 5.9s for presentation. For the moment she moved into first place.

Bobek's tears had expressed her disappointment; Chen-Lu's were tears of joy.

Exotic looking in multicolored sequins and an elaborate hairdo, Surya Bonaly took to the ice, a determined expression on her pretty face.

She began her program with confidence, sailing into a knock-'em-dead lineup of triple jumps, most in combination, plus *two* consecutive double axels. The time and energy she'd spent practicing on home ice, where she'd been given the keys to the local ice rink, were in evidence.

Bonaly wasn't lacking in athleticism or charisma, but a problem lurked in the overall concept of her program: it didn't seem to have any structure.

All the elements were powerfully presented, one after another, but with no particular flow. The moves seemed randomly strung together, there was no inner tension, and her program wasn't telling a story or building to a climax.

Bonaly also utilized a peculiar, gymnastic-type of technique in several jumps, particularly the triple lutz, where she appeared to be on the flat of her blade, not the back outside edge, in her too-long preparatory entrance.

But she remained on her feet, and performed a difficult variation of the camel spin, grabbing onto the skate blade of her free leg, then raising her leg to almost touch the back of her head.

The judges had plenty to reflect on in the couple of moments available to them to decide on Bonaly's marks. She usually came out ahead, and tonight, as usual, the crowd responded enthusiastically to her efforts.

Chen-Lu and her coach had watched the performance from the sidelines and waited anxiously to see Bonaly's scores.

Chen-Lu was still ahead! She sobbed. "I'm so happy— thank you—"

But there was one more skater who still had to perform.

People sat forward in their seats. How would fourteen-year-old Michelle Kwan fit into this equation? Backstage, she, too, seemed apprehensive. Dressed in red and pink, a sprinkling of sequins adding sparkle to her costume, she wore little makeup and no lipstick.

Frank Carroll, wearing an expression of confidence and determination, spoke a few final words to his student as she was about to take to the ice. She responded with a smile of acknowledgment, eager to begin.

"Going in, I was nervous," she later admitted, "but the audience calmed me down."

An appealing expression on her face accompanied her first move. Building from there, she skated the best she had to date, technically and artistically, infusing her performance with spirit and energy. She was exhilarated as one element segued "effortlessly" into another, first a huge double axel, later a second one in combination with a double toe, then a triple flip, and a beautiful spin combination. . . .

Cheers from the audience spurred her on. Her second triple lutz was even better than the first. A radiant smile lit up her face.

When it was over, Kwan received a rousing ovation. People were on their feet. The youngster was overwhelmed. "Oh my God, what did I just do!" she exclaimed to herself.

She remained center ice, breathing hard, tears of relieved tension rolling down her cheeks.

Even Frank Carroll, adept at concealing his feelings when in the public eye, seemed emotional.

"Wonderful," he told Michelle as she skated off the ice.

"Thank you," she said, barely audibly. The intense but civilized interplay between them was a lesson in building a dream on the proper foundation.

After the refusal of some judges to acknowledge the quality of her short program, it was anybody's guess what the official reception would be for her effort tonight in the long program.

Mission accomplished? Yes and no. Incredibly, there would be no medal for Michelle! She received 5.7s to 5.9 for technical merit; one inexplicable 5.6, up to 5.9 for artistic impression. Three judges had ranked Chen-Lu first in the long, and her total overall scores enabled her to become world champion.

Long-suffering Surya Bonaly won Silver; she seemed reconciled to the present and hopeful about the future.

Nicole Bobek was elated with her Bronze Medal. She'd proven to herself that the negative publicity about her private life hadn't ruined this event for her, "didn't affect me in any way. I went out there and skated my best."

Michelle's fine showing had affected the dynamics of the judging; her beating Bobek in the long caused Nicole to drop to third and enabled Bonaly to pull up to second.

Kwan's final placement: fourth.

Did she believe she deserved a medal? "It doesn't matter," she said. "In my heart, I feel great."

CHAPTER TEN

~~

Breakthrough

Frank Carroll evaluated "official" skating world reaction to his pupil. "She had great jumps and people said, 'That's a good little skater,' " he later recalled. While that was a positive start, Carroll had something else in mind, a reaction that would not even mention her jumps. Instead, they would exclaim, "That's beautiful. That's a pleasure to watch."

Despite failing to win a medal, Michelle had made her mark on the world stage. But she also had realized "there was something wrong." The next goal was set: "to improve on what they [the judges] were looking for—a more mature look," she said.

"They want a ladies' world champion, not a girls' world champion," said Frank Carroll.

"Maybe [the judges] thought I was too young," said Michelle. "I think that had a lot to do with it, but I really don't care. It wasn't up to me. It's up to everybody else to decide whether I'm first or last. I did my best and was excited afterward and I didn't care where I finished."

Michelle felt a glow of satisfaction. Her father and Mr. Carroll were pleased. Danny Kwan was delighted to grant a request made by his daughter: Michelle was dying to attend the wedding, in Cleveland, of her skating friends Jenni Meno and Todd Sand, U.S. pair champions. (Twenty-six-year-old Meno and thirty-three-year-old Sand trained alongside Kwan at Lake Arrowhead, and Frank Carroll had been helping them with their triple jumps.)

Michelle's other wish, which her father was considering: she wanted him to buy her a boat.

Her agent had negotiated a deal for Michelle to appear in the prestigious Campbell's Soups Tour of World Figure Skating Champions, and she was looking forward to it. The opportunity to develop her skills at performing for audiences without the pressure of a panel of judges grading her every move was a godsend. She was also looking forward to spending downtime with friends, of being that "normal" kid she indeed was.

Already a plan was taking shape regarding Michelle's image—something daring and dramatic. Only time would tell if it was feasible.

Working alongside the finest skaters in the world, playing to mostly sold-out houses in dozens of cities throughout the country, Michelle had a terrific time on tour. Her program to the soundtrack of the film *Pocahontas* was a consistent showstopper.

With her friends Brian Boitano and Elvis Stojko, she worked on her triple axel. The men had long since mastered the notoriously tricky move, which had a habit of disappearing just when one felt secure with it!

Still, Kwan didn't neglect her formal education; even on tour, in the privacy of her hotel room, she made sure she didn't fall behind in her studies. She was taking courses in French, English, history, algebra, and biology at the level of a high-school sophomore. Mandarin, a complex dialect of the Chinese language, intrigued her. So far, she mastered two sentences: "I'm very hungry" and "I'm very tired."

She would one day make an interesting comment regarding her future on ice: "I always tell myself I'm not going to do this until I'm thirty. That's way too long. If you can't show your best on the ice, why show it? I want to be the best and walk out. I don't want to be skating when I'm going downhill."

Still, the only direction Michelle was headed in now was up. Regarding the dilemma of somehow turning her into an "adult" for the purposes of competition, there was a solution. But would the Kwans go along with it? It was obvious Frank Carroll was going to have to do a lot of convincing.

Fifteen-year-old Michelle Kwan as Salome? The character from the Bible? In fact, according to historians, the young woman noted for performing the Dance of the Seven Veils was around Michelle's age, and perhaps even younger. An interesting point of fact: the Bible never identifies Salome by name. It was Oscar Wilde, in his play *Salome*, who designated the character as having the name of "Salome."

> *But when Herod's birthday was kept, the daughter of Herodias danced before them and pleased Herod. . . .*
> *Whereupon he promised with an oath to give her whatsoever she would ask.*
> *And she, being before instructed by her mother, said, Give me here John Baptist's head. . . .*
>
> New Testament, Gospel of Matthew, 14

Was Carroll *serious* about Michelle's depiction? In addition to special costuming, Michelle would have to wear heavy makeup, and Michelle's parents felt that was out of the question!

Carroll had to explain that if Michelle was appearing in a ballet, she'd have to look the part, wouldn't she? Makeup was an essential tool; "it's part of the schtick," he argued. He knew full well that Michelle's Chinese background decreed, "You don't wear makeup at that age."

"We're not talking school exams," he continued. "We're performing in front of thousands of people."

Danny Kwan was fearful; he didn't want Michelle to "overdo it." But he realized she was growing up, becoming a young woman. A practical man, he reasoned one had to go with the flow.

Michelle shared Carroll's vision. Her plan of how to become one of the best "included her personal look, moves, and music," recalled Carroll.

This decision was to prove a journey of self-discovery for Michelle. Her trusted choreographer, Lori Nichol, undertook the task of creating an atmosphere in which she gently coaxed Michelle into tapping in to and utilizing her creative instincts.

There must be nothing fake out there; it must be honest for it to work. Lori Nichol had faith in her pupil, and vice versa. Nothing must get in the way of Michelle striving for a direct emotional reaction in her skating.

In the past, Carroll and Nichol simply presented Michelle ("she's so easygoing") with music and choreography, and she simply expressed her approval and said, "Let's go."

Now, for the first time, Michelle became actively

involved in *all* aspects of creating her program. At the outset, asked how she would interpret sections of the music, Michelle's first responses were, well, this is how so-and-so would do it, this is how Oksana would do it. . . .

How would *you* do it? Nichol wanted to know. They pressed on. Very late one night the moment came when Michelle at last understood what Lori had been driving at.

Michelle indicated at last how *she* would do it, and it was an emotional awakening—her opportunity to "let herself go," to bring a genuine maturity to her work.

The program took shape, and the day finally came when there was a run-through. The performance brought tears to Lori Nichol's eyes, and she paid Kwan the ultimate compliment: "You are an artist."

Michelle gratefully concurred. "Yes," she said quietly, "I am an artist."

Needless to say, no particular movement implying the beheading of John the Baptist would be made. "So we had to make a little different ending," Michelle quipped.

Plus her ponytail had to go. "I don't think it's the image she's trying to portray anymore," noted Carroll. Her mom and sister, Karen, helped with the metamorphosis, and Oksana Baiul, no novice when it came to makeovers, offered Michelle some suggestions and advice on her makeup.

Worries remained. Ridiculous as it sounded, might the "new" Michelle, portraying Salome, possibly be perceived in some quarters as vulgar? Was the concept too far out?

Carroll was adamant. "I don't think it's vulgar. I think

I'm a person with taste," he declared. "So are her parents." So was Michelle! "I don't think we'd do something that wasn't tasteful."

Michelle, her mom, and Karen experimented with a new hairstyle. When a final decision was made, it took half an hour to fashion her long black hair into the Salome look. She had to braid, wrap, and sew the "do" in place.

Would it all work?

Michelle adopted aspects of the "look" for practice sessions. The skating world would have to be prepared, in stages, for what was coming.

"Grooming shows you care, that you want to do everything the best. You have to look the part," said Carroll.

The concept, and Michelle's interpretation of it, took off. It was exciting to be presented with the opportunity to express herself, to release her imagination through creating a character within the framework of her skating.

As choreographer/dancer Ann Reinking has said, "Movement isn't really movement—it's acting."

As Salome, Michelle would act as one element flowed into another. She strove to create an illusion, letting nothing disrupt the flow of the characterization or the choreography.

A daunting prospect for a fifteen-year-old? Others her age had accomplished similar miracles in other venues. It was a question of talent, not of life experience. A sheltered fourteen-year-old country singer named LeAnn Rimes was soon to burst on the country-music scene with a smash hit rendition of an adult love song, "Blue."

Where had a child like LeAnn, as carefully reared and

nurtured as Michelle, acquired the knowledge and under-standing to infuse the lyrics with such meaning? She explained that she simply used the feelings she'd experienced within her own universe and applied them to the lyrics—her imagination and talent did the rest.

Decades earlier, another prodigy, thirteen-year-old Judy Garland, accomplished the same feat, using her extraordinary vocal and histrionic gifts to effectively interpret adult music.

As "Salome" took shape, all concerned sensed they were onto something special.

At this point Michelle's life offered less time than ever for diversions. "We've all agreed skating comes first, second, and third," Shep Goldberg had said. "Nothing should conflict with skating or be a negative."

Michelle was rarely without her teddy-bear knapsack, in which she stored her personal items. She giggled about boys and had popular screen favorites: Tom Cruise, Brad Pitt, and especially the star of *Baywatch*, David Hasselhoff. When Kwan and Hasselhoff finally met (another "perk" when one was a leader in one's field), Michelle recalled that she almost fainted!

Detroit, Michigan, automobile capital of the world and fifth largest city in the United States, was to be the launching site of Skate America International in October—and, it was hoped, the official launching of the "new" Michelle.

The first Olympic-style event of the 1995–1996 season, it was one of five related competitions (called the "Champion Series") to be held in various cities throughout the world. The purpose: to enable skaters to win thousands of dollars in prize money without forfeiting their Olympic eligibility.

Some expected this to be Nicole Bobek's event, her opportunity to reemerge and set the standard for the new season. Only nine months had passed since she had won Nationals, eight months since winning Bronze at Worlds.

Besides, waves of gossip about Kwan had washed over the skating community, to the effect that the envelope *had* been pushed too far. Predictions were that Michelle and her "team" would find themselves facing a negative backlash.

Michelle skated out onto the ice to begin her new short program, "Spanish Medley."

"Who is that?" people wanted to know.

It was a mild shock to behold Michelle's new persona. Gone was the perky young teen with the ponytail and the eager attitude; in her place was a strikingly dramatic creature who exuded a sense of mystery.

"Off the ice, she's a playful fifteen-year-old," noted an insider. "When she hits the ice, she's all business."

Her music began. Immediately it was obvious: the line, stretch, and flow of her movements had reached a rare level of polish, one that inspired a hush in the audience: don't intrude on the moment, let it happen.

Her form was flawless as she built to the finale of the routine, the flamenco beat throbbing in the music as her flashing blades traversed the ice.

She ended with an incredible combination spin (always keeping her toes pointed—it was amazing how many top skaters ignored this very basic proper position). Rising from a sit spin, she took hold of her free leg and extended it in a ballet-kick position, throwing her head backward as she continued to spin.

An artist was coming into her own.

Then came the long program; the moment of truth had arrived. The Salome costume was a masterpiece of illusion, glittering with brilliants on a combination deep purple and flesh-colored fabric. Michelle's team had worked almost as hard on creating it as on creating the routine, and the effect was dazzling. Her makeup now included a silver sequin pasted at the corner of each eye.

The power and seductiveness of the program were in evidence from her opening stance. A dynamic stillness was combined with a flowing, floating feeling of lightness. The Far East–flavored choreography, merely hinted at in Michelle's previous programs over the years, was now dominant, blending and holding all elements together.

Michelle brought something of herself to the audience, came alive in this number. Her performance was spellbinding.

Her spiral sequences had developed to breathtaking heights, in extension, line, and control. Here was a presentation that was exciting to watch even if she didn't jump! It had the impact of a three-act play, fused in theme and plot and building to a resounding climax.

This was Kwan's *breakthrough*. The gamble had worked—Michelle had carried it off, although whether or not "Salome" would win acceptance throughout the jealousy-infested, politics-ridden skating community remained to be seen.

Michelle herself was happy with the results. She liked the new look, the costumes. "I got the perfect costumes," she said. "I think everything's perfect now. [From now on] it all depends on how I skate." During the course of the season, there would be refinements and improvements in Michelle's Salome performance as she grew more relaxed presenting the program before an audience.

Nicole Bobek encountered an opposite experience at the event: in her long program, the blond beauty failed to complete a single triple jump.

Had old habits resurfaced? Were her training methods, or lack of them, back in her life? Was a recent knee injury responsible?

Bobek offered no excuses. She said she'd had a bad warm-up and got so shook up that she couldn't get her feet under her. Michelle won the competition.

Rumors were surfacing that Tonya Harding wanted to reenter competitive ranks. Frank Carroll was quoted as saying that if this were to occur, he'd be sure to place Michelle in a suit of armor.

In the meantime the Champion Series competitions would take Kwan to Canada, Germany, and back to the U.S., where a team (Non-Champion Series) competition was to be held in Philadelphia.

For the 1995 Christmas season in New York, there would be the fabled tree-lighting ceremony at Rockefeller Center in early December. Michelle had been asked to be the star attraction of the ice show that was traditionally a key element in the festivities. It was quite an honor—the eyes of the world were always focused on this happy event.

But amid all the activity and excitement of that fall of 1995, a dreadful tragedy occurred. It happened on

November 20, and on hearing the news, one almost felt unable to accept its reality. It couldn't be true—everyone had such admiration and respect for him. Such a thing simply couldn't happen to a young skater in the prime of his life!

Sergei Grinkov, twenty-eight years old, two-time Olympic pairs champion with his wife, Ekaterina Gordeyeva, was dead. He hadn't fallen; he didn't take a spill.

Practicing a routine with his wife at the Lake Placid Olympic Center in Lake Placid, New York, he was about to lift her, but didn't. He felt dizzy and held on to the barrier. "He lay down, very quietly," recalled his wife, and she kept asking him what was happening.

It was a fatal heart attack, totally unexpected. There had been no history of serious medical problems. Sergei and Katya were the couple who had everything. "They skated for each other. You could feel them connect," said Natalya Dubova, a friend. Another commented, "Their hearts seemed to beat at the same time."

A devastated Scott Hamilton said, "This is an enormous shock. This is the healthiest person I know. He took care of himself."

The Grinkovs had inspired Michelle and her fellow skaters on all fronts: not only were they perfect together on ice, but they had a relationship that seemed close to perfect. Their child, Daria ("Dasha"), was a blond charmer, a radiant being who was somehow a facsimile of both parents.

Now Daria's father was dead. Skaters would approach the competitive events of the current season with heavy hearts.

*   *   *

But life had to go on.

In New York for the Rockefeller Center tree-lighting event, Michelle would be skating on outdoor ice. The rink was considerably smaller than Olympic size and didn't really lend itself to a full complement of triples, yet the ambience easily compensated for any physical shortcomings.

Famous throughout the world for its towering skyscrapers, Rockefeller Center is a "city within a city," the buildings among the finest examples of modern American architecture, abounding with outstanding contemporary sculpture and painting.

The huge statue of Prometheus, freshly gold-leafed, reclined on his golden pedestal like a gleaming angel watching over the ice rink. The giant Christmas tree, decorated with more than twenty-five thousand twinkling lights the color of the rainbow, rose almost ten stories from street level.

Scaffolding had been erected all around the upper and lower regions of the rink to accommodate TV personnel and equipment. Rink manager Carol Olsen and comanager David Meltzer always managed to keep everything functioning smoothly amid the never-ending bustle of activity.

The outdoor ice, often "harder" and more brittle than indoor ice, where the atmosphere could be controlled, was maintained in peak condition—no simple task. Depending on the weather conditions, it might be far more difficult for a skater to grip an edge; sometimes one had to contend with sudden strong gusts of wind that created additional problems by throwing a spin off-center or impeding the flow of a jump.

On this occasion, it was associate coach Evelyn Kramer who worked with Michelle on her presentation. It was fascinating to observe the subtle give-and-take between teacher and pupil. Kramer, a New Yorker now head-quartered at Lake Arrowhead and a dynamic, attractive, and often outspoken woman who'd been a first-class skater herself when Michelle's age, was very low key when offering suggestions. Often, Kramer would simply tilt her body a certain way, indicating to Michelle how she might adjust her posture on takeoffs or landings that were troubling her.

Kwan wasn't accustomed to either outdoor ice or the small surface, and seemed to react to Kramer's sugges-tions impassively. However, she proceeded to implement every one.

Her dad paced nervously on the sidelines. If an out-sider was to be asked if it were father or daughter who had a case of the jitters, one would not have pointed to the daughter.

Off the ice, Michelle was friendly, intelligent, and seemed to be having a fine time. She was delighted to be in New York, looked forward to seeing some sights, and always had a smile and a good word for admirers.

At practice the day of the tree-lighting ceremonies, Michelle was having trouble with her double axel and chose to omit it for the actual performance. At the last minute she substituted a single axel. The on-site crowd and television viewers couldn't have cared less; all were entranced by her graceful, light-as-air style.

For Michelle, it was then on to the 1996 Nationals in San Jose, California, the Championship Series Final in Paris, and the World Championships in England. All would test Michelle's mettle.

CHAPTER ELEVEN

~~~

Enter Tara

Slated to compete at senior level at Nationals for the first time, Tara Lipinski was two years younger than Michelle Kwan. Her parents, Patricia ("Pat") and Jack, had been high-school sweethearts in their native New Jersey. Jack enrolled in the Stevens Institute of Technology and hoped to become a chemical engineer. His relationship with Pat progressed to the altar, and the couple were wed on May 4, 1974.

Tara was born in Philadelphia on June 10, 1982, the year that Prince Charles and Princess Diana celebrated their first wedding anniversary. *Raiders of the Lost Ark* and *E.T.* were the big movies, and Rosalynn Sumners and Elaine Zayak were the dominant ladies in U.S. figure skating.

Tara's home environment was not in any way sports-oriented, although her dad was a good natural athlete. He was career-oriented, however, and chose to work in the oil industry, joining the Texaco Corporation. Pat entered the workforce as an executive secretary. In 1988, after attending night school, Jack earned his law degree, and by 1991, he was named a vice-president of the Houston-based Coastal Corporation.

* * *

As children, Michelle and Tara shared the same dream: to become skating champions. Although Jack Lipinski has recalled "no huge aspirations" along those lines, there have been accounts that Tara's goal of mounting the podium had formed in her mind by age two!

Her inspiration was said to have been the medal ceremonies at the 1984 Summer Olympics, which she saw on television. These motivated tiny Tara to improvise her own podium—a large plastic salad bowl—and bestow her own "medal."

A family neighbor, Aurora Polutan, has recalled that Tara was the smallest kid on the block in their Sewell, New Jersey, neighborhood. And the most active: she was always in motion, on foot or otherwise, and when her tricycle was traded in for a bike, "she pedaled as fast as she could go."

It was roller skating, not figure skating, that initially captured the child's imagination. "Once she got into it," remembered Mrs. Polutan, "we saw less of her because she spent every free moment skating and taking lessons at the rink."

Michelle had won her first competition on ice by age seven, and Tara's early victories on wheels occurred around the same age. The transition to ice happened swiftly, although when her parents first observed her on figure skates, and saw her fall repeatedly, they were certain that she would never become an ice skater.

But her roller-skating technique enabled the youngster to begin jumping and spinning on ice almost immediately, and to the present day, Tara's powerful double axel reflects her roller-skating background. Rather than stepping up into the jump, as figure skaters are taught to do, reaching peak height and *then* rotating, Tara immediately begins the two and a half revolutions as she lifts off the ice.

Just as the Kwans faced financial hardship and a dramatic change in lifestyle in order to underwrite their daughter's dream, so did Pat and Jack Lipinski. Tara was an only child, however, so the burden was less complex if no less heavy. Indeed, at one point it became necessary to refinance the mortgage on the Lipinski home, and at one point to pay for groceries with credit cards.

Mom and Dad Lipinski, like Estella and Danny Kwan, had to forgo the conventional husband-and-wife living arrangements; Pat went to be with Tara at her training facility while Jack remained in Houston, where the family had moved because of a job offer. Tara's skating bills were mounting and Jack wanted the family, which included five beloved dogs, to have a home base.

Pat Lipinski, an attractive, intelligent, soft-spoken, and friendly woman with blond hair and blue eyes, observed the intensity of her daughter's dedication to skating with awe. "It's a shame they have to do this at such a young age," she said, but it was obvious that this was what Tara wanted to do with all her heart.

Like Michelle, Tara began attracting attention early on. At age eleven, the age when Michelle had been relocated to the Lake Arrowhead training center, Tara began training at the University of Delaware ice arena, a prestigious venue for promising talents.

Tara was aware that her mother was lonely and missed Jack, and so did she! "But I'd give my daughter anything," declared Pat. "She loves it. And we're seeing results." She realized it would be traumatic for Tara if she put a halt to the whole endeavor, and couldn't stop visualizing the consequences. "For the rest of my life, I'd have to sit around and think, 'What if, what if?' "

It was a situation the Kwans could intimately relate to.

Tara's education, like Michelle's, was soon in the hands of tutors (two hours a day each morning). A skating career was a huge, costly gamble on all fronts. At least the work ethic that was required, and the building of self-confidence, would be valuable for Tara and Michelle no matter what paths they chose later in life.

Tara dabbled with other interests; she reportedly twirled a baton, and played basketball, and the piano. She even, on occasion, modeled, her beaming smile clicking on the instant the lens pointed in her direction.

According to Jeff DiGregorio, her coach at the time, Tara's jumping ability at age twelve far surpassed Katarina Witt's and Kristi Yamaguchi's at the same age.

Michelle, at fourteen, had already been runner-up in Nationals, been to the Olympics, and competed in Worlds at the time twelve-year-old Tara's goal was set: "I want to go to the Olympics and win."

Was she giving up a "normal" childhood to pursue her ambition? Lipinski and Kwan seemed to share the same outlook: "Look at what all the other kids are missing out on," said Tara. In her case, nonskating friends dropped away because she had no time to devote to them. Just as Danny Kwan had insisted on a proper education for Michelle, Pat was adamant that Tara maintain an "A" average in her studies. And if a life on ice was Tara's unalterable choice, her mom wouldn't tolerate any sloughing off at practice.

Mrs. Lipinski drove her daughter to the rink every day, where Tara's routine consisted of landing each jump at least five times "clean." Any mistakes and the move would be repeated until it was correct.

"She works really hard," her mother noted understandingly, "but I want her to work to the max because we're giving up our lives for this."

Like the Kwans, the Lipinskis weren't wasting their time.

Tara was entering senior competition with a respectable résumé. In 1994, at age twelve, she'd won the junior title at the U.S. Olympic Festival in St. Louis, and in the Blue Swords event in Germany. The previous year, she'd placed second at the National Juniors in Anchorage, Alaska, and fourth in the World Junior Championships in Budapest, Hungary. At one competition she included a triple flip that she'd been practicing only for two weeks.

Like Michelle, she was becoming a world traveler and seasoned competitor at an early age. She was looking forward to the upcoming contest for U.S. Gold.

CHAPTER TWELVE

Do You Know the Way to San Jose?

San Jose, California, located fifty miles south of San Francisco, was the setting for the 1996 U.S. National Championships.

On the evening of the men's long program, an unforgettable event occurred. Michelle, her fellow skaters, and the SRO crowd cheered on San Jose hometown boy Rudy Galindo, former pairs partner of Kristi Yamaguchi, as he defied all predictions and zeroed in on the Senior Men's title. He pulled out all the stops, electrified the crowd, and won a thunderous standing ovation—plus two perfect 6.0s for presentation—and the Gold Medal. A surprised Todd Eldredge placed second.

Michelle's pals Jenni Meno and Todd Sand won the pairs competition, despite the fact that Jenni had taken a spill on one of their "throw" jumps.

Shelby Lyons, thirteen and a half years old, with virtually no experience as a pairs skater, was newly teamed with an older partner, Brian Wells, and to everyone's surprise the couple placed third. "It's our goal to reach the Olympics," said Wells.

* * *

Galindo had provided a jolt of excitement and drama, and the ladies' competition promised more of the same. Karen Kwan, now seventeen, was competing once again, and the media was eager for something to report— sibling rivalry, jealousy; the tabloid menu offered many possibilities.

However, since the sisters were obviously best friends, another angle was discussed: what a story it would make if both Kwans landed in the top three; after all, anything was possible in today's skating world!

Still, the big contest was supposed to take place between defending champion Nicole Bobek and Michelle. Everyone was talking about Michelle's "transformation," and she was psyched for the challenge.

Nicole Bobek was nursing an injury—tendonitis in one of her ankles. However, she seemed eager and willing to compete. Bobek's current coach, Barbara Roles Williams, was her ninth in nine years. Even Frank Carroll, back in 1989, had filled these shoes. And despite speculation on Bobek's physical condition from various quarters, her warm-up sessions were satisfactory.

The view from the top had offered poor visibility for Nicole. After last year's victory, everyone had wanted to sign her for shows, tours, photo shoots. Everything "exploded," she later explained, adding forlornly: "In a way, it was all too much."

Along with Todd Eldredge, she'd played a twenty-city tour of *The Nutcracker* in the month preceding Nationals, and was criticized in official circles for not taking that month to train. Over the past year her skating hadn't improved. Gossips declared the ankle injury happened because of the bad judgment she'd exercised in opting for the tour (and the reported $90,000 it had earned her).

Depending on one's point of view, Bobek was either not in touch with her alleged ambition to maintain champion status, or she was simply a young person desperately in need of motivation.

Bobek went on to skate a respectable short program. Michelle's "Spanish Medley," however, was a sensation, and the lady in red won first place in the short. Tonia Kwiatkowski achieved second, and Bobek third.

In view of her injury, and third-place showing in the short program, it was assumed Nicole would settle this year for simply making the world team. It was a disturbing situation for the girl who said her dream had been "to dazzle and defend the title."

In fourth place was last year's National Junior champion, Sydney Vogel. Tara Lipinski, who'd been runner-up to Vogel in that event, was fifth, followed by Karen Kwan.

Because Tara, built like a ten-year-old, propelled herself over the ice with such speed, there were remarks that her Energizer batteries were changed like clockwork before each performance. She didn't seem nervous or intimidated, exclaimed veterans, because what thirteen-year-old would be? Tara was too young for nerves to have taken hold. All youths were fearless. ("I think she was too young to be intimidated last year," Frank Carroll had said about Michelle back in 1994. "At thirteen, there is no fear. As you get older, it gets tougher.")

Lipinski had changed coaches, and Richard Callaghan, Todd Eldredge's coach and Nicole Bobek's former coach, was now in charge.

* * *

The warm-up preceding the long program was fascinating. Michelle was as sleek and agile as a jungle cat. Tara was skimming the surface as fast as a flash of lightning. Bobek had been warned by her coach not to jump the triple lutz and to avoid straining her ankle; save the jump for the actual program, she was told. Nicole ignored the advice, and afterward there were tears in her eyes. She seemed in pain and conferred with Roles, her coach; earlier, the skater had declined a pain-relieving, association-approved shot of cortisone.

The skating order: Sydney Vogel, Michelle, Nicole, Tara, Karen Kwan, and Tonia Kwiatkowski.

Once again, Kwiatkowski—this was her ninth time competing in the senior division—could be the spoiler. She was well equipped to assume the role.

As we've said, the first to skate is always at a disadvantage, because the judges leave "room" in the scores for subsequent skaters. In this case, it was the Alaskan Sydney Vogel, wearing a red costume embroidered with silver sequins, who had this dubious honor. She performed with spirit and skill, adeptly and professionally. But Vogel's technical marks, 5.2 to 5.6, and artistic scores, 5.3 to 5.5, left plenty of room.

Michelle, dazzling in her Salome makeup and costume, her grandparents' good-luck charm momentarily tucked into her neckline, absorbed Frank Carroll's final words before skating to center ice.

"Be aggressive on your first jump," he always advised her, and after her spellbinding opening steps, she launched her triple-lutz-double-toe combination with speed and power. For her next combination, the ultra-difficult triple-toe-triple-toe, she built up the necessary speed (a shade too fast or too slow could be disastrous), tapped with her toe pick into the ice for takeoff, and landed perfectly.

A triple flip, triple loop, and second triple lutz were performed confidently, all woven into the fabric of her choreography.

Onlookers held their breath as she skated the final half minute of her program. The tension in the music was matched by Michelle's moves; all were building toward the final, precisely-timed-to-the-music double axel.

The moment came . . . and she "singled" the jump! An instant later the program was over. Michelle acknowledged the roar of applause from the crowd with a deep, extraordinarily graceful bow.

When she stood, she playfully berated herself, hitting her head lightly for missing that last jump. But she hadn't fallen or left out a key element; she'd performed the double axel earlier. There would be no deductions.

Frank Carroll hugged her as Michelle skated to kiss-and-cry just as news was being received that Nicole Bobek was withdrawing from the competition because of her injury. Her ankle was badly swollen, and the team doctor was fearful of permanent injury if she performed.

Tara Lipinski, a tiny figure in red, took to the ice as all waited for Michelle Kwan's marks to flash on the screen: 5.8 to 5.9 for technical, 5.8 to 5.9 for artistic merit. All judges had placed her first: it was virtually impossible to knock her off her perch.

Danny and Estella Kwan, in the stands, wore expressions of deep relief and satisfaction.

* * *

Skating to the movie soundtracks of *Speed* and Barbra Streisand's *The Prince of Tides*, Tara Lipinski appeared calm and confident. She'd performed her program all the way through, from beginning to end, time after time after time, all jumps included, whenever she practiced.

She was too tiny in stature to have the stretch, line, and form that characterized Michelle Kwan's efforts. Lipinski's style was totally different: fast, perky, and exact. When she began the slow, "quiet" section of her program, the expression on her face seemed, understandably, that of a child emulating an adult portraying emotion.

Among the elements she performed were double axels, a triple flip, and a triple loop, but she'd also included a surprise. She attempted a triple-salchow-triple-loop combination . . . and fell hard on the second jump.

Quick as a flash she was back on her feet, and to compensate for the failed jump, a few seconds later she improvised another triple salchow, this time in combination with a double axel. A show-stopping illusion back camel spin, very powerfully performed, ended the program.

Some members of the audience sprang to their feet, applauding and shouting their approval of Lipinski's efforts.

She was awarded 5.4 to 5.8 for technical merit, but presentation brought a lower set of marks: 5.2 to 5.5. The judges had appreciated her technical proficiency, but saw the lack of maturity.

As all waited for Tara's scores, Karen Kwan, looking lovely in white chiffon glittering with silver-sequin trim, skated onto the ice. Performing to the soundtrack of the film *The Mission*, she displayed a style that was not a carbon copy of her sister's or of anyone else's. She skated with sophistication and flow, and most of her elements were completed with confidence and strength.

Afterward, in kiss-and-cry, she sat with Michelle and Frank Carroll, the sisters laughing and joking. Karen's scores flashed on the screen: 5.2 to 5.3 for technical merit, 5.3 to 5.8 for artistic presentation. Michelle was thrilled with Karen's 5.8.

But why had Karen's technical marks been so low? What were the major deductions for? It's often hard to know. In figure skating, once marks are awarded, they are never changed.

At this point in the competition Tonia Kwiatkowski saw a window of opportunity open for her. Her facial expression conveyed her attitude: pure determination. She was going to *fight* for this one.

She delivered six triples, some in combination, as she skated a workmanlike, mistake-free program she said was her birthday gift to her coach of sixteen years, Carol Heiss Jenkins.

Her efforts were admirable. There was pure joy on her face, and that of her coach, as the judges unanimously placed her second, their technical scores ranging from 5.7 to 5.8, presentation scores from 5.7 to 5.9.

But Michelle Kwan, at fifteen, had become the youngest U.S. national champion since Peggy Fleming in 1964 (Fleming had been three weeks younger), and the third youngest in history. It must have seemed very dreamlike, walking through the people backstage congratulating her, skating to the podium, and having the medal placed around her neck. All like a dream yet excitingly real.

* * *

But the competition wasn't over yet. There was an important decision to make, although everyone was certain how it would be made. *Of course* Bobek would be permitted to compete in Worlds; after all, she was last year's national champion and had won Bronze at Worlds.

The International Management Committee of the United States Figure Skating Association had the power to determine who would represent the U.S.A. in world competition. Usually they chose the top three skaters, but Nicole Bobek's withdrawal from competition had created a problem. Still, there was ample precedent for allowing an injured skater, forced to withdraw from Nationals, to be named a member of the team. Nancy Kerrigan, in '94, was the most recent example.

But Bobek was bypassed; she would not be allowed to compete in Worlds. Once again, an official decision by figure-skating officials caused ripples of resentment and waves of controversy in the skating community.

In the meantime Nicole had unwittingly paved the way for at least one of her fellow competitors to move up a notch. Tara Lipinski, in third place, would have been bumped off the world team to accommodate Nicole; the thirteen-year-old would have had to wait an additional year.

Already being described as "a very ambitious child," Tara was remarkably poised in fielding the usual questions from the press. While many of her peers had high-pitched voices and garbled their words, Tara spoke clearly, articulately, and remarkably intelligently.

Now that she was Bronze Medalist and a member of the world team, had it all been "easy"?

No, Tara replied, it had not been "easy," but she'd wanted to skate well and have fun, and she felt she had accomplished these goals. She seemed not the slightest bit surprised that events had taken the turn they had.

Michelle, always gracious, stated simply that she'd worked really hard and was happy and grateful she'd done so well. There was celebrating over the fact that she'd be entering Worlds as U.S. national champion, an honor, all concurred, that was very well deserved.

CHAPTER THIRTEEN

Skater Beware

Paris. The "city of light," "the capital of the world," and arguably the world's greatest center for art, learning, culture, and pleasure.

In an era when anyone in the public eye is in danger of being assaulted, it was here that Michelle Kwan had her close encounter. She had received a death threat. Over the past year, through a series of persistent phone calls and letters, a disturbed person, reportedly a resident of Paris, had been trying to get in touch with her. Frank Carroll later described him as a sick person, a strange little man who had written many letters, made many phone calls.

His attempts had grown "very very aggressive," recalled Carroll, so much so that the FBI had become involved. The person had been very persistent in tracking Kwan down, contacting the U.S. State Department, the U.S. and French skating federations, and even Michelle's Lake Arrowhead training center.

Michelle was informed of the problem, told about the letters. She remained unperturbed. The man was under close scrutiny by French authorities. "They know where he is every minute," said Frank Carroll, who, along with

Danny Kwan and the powers that be, made sure Michelle was well protected.

When Michelle arrived in Paris to compete at a Champion Series event, security was tighter than ever at the arena. She was fighting a bronchial infection, which had wreaked havoc on her performances at the Centennial on Ice competition in St. Petersburg, Russia, the previous week.

Michelle had managed to squeeze in a bit of sightseeing in St. Petersburg, scene of the first World Figure Skating Championship (for men only) one hundred years earlier. The city's wide boulevards and beautiful palaces dating back to the days of the czars were awesome to behold, and the many bridges crossing narrow canals and connecting the various parts of the city added to its allure.

But Michelle was having problems on the ice. Among other things, the timing on her jumps was suffering because of her illness. She finished third in the competition.

In Paris, everyone marveled at how someone so young could thrive under such pressure. Michelle was now fighting a bad cold, and her practice sessions were alarming to watch: she missed jumps and took bad falls. But instead of curtailing her schedule, she increased the number of hours she was spending on the ice. One had to admire her dedication and determination.

In the champion series event, she delivered a flawed short program, which included a fall on a triple toe loop, and finished third. Sometimes a skater goes into a kind of shock when she has missed a big jump, and the rest of her performance suffers for it. But Michelle wasn't flustered or despondent after this setback. Her marks reflected the gaffe, 5.1 to 5.3 for required elements, including a mandatory deduction of four-tenths of a point for the failed jump. Presentation scores soared up to 5.5 to 5.8.

She discussed the mistake *sotto voce* in kiss-and-cry with Frank Carroll and, after the scores appeared, smiled and acknowledged the applause.

Chen-Lu had the lead.

Although she didn't expect to win the Paris competition, Michelle's performance in the long program was dynamic and exciting. She was the only skater in the ladies' division to include a triple triple-toe-loop combination, and she executed it flawlessly. Her second triple lutz turned into a double midair, and she two-footed the landing, but her final double axel was a beauty, timed perfectly as always to the shimmering violin figures in the music.

When informed that the Gold Medal (plus a $50,000 first prize) was hers (Chen-Lu had had a bad day and finished fourth), Michelle was shocked. What was the champion thinking about while performing her program? She said she hadn't been thinking about winning, but had simply concentrated on what she had to do.

She acknowledged that it had been a tough week and that she hadn't been in top shape, but was determined to get through it and had "rallied" for the long program.

"She forgets the past and moves forward," observed Dorothy Hamill admiringly. Hamill understood all too well the harrowing pitfalls of a champion's goldfish-bowl existence.

Kwan was learning to deal with a world of incessant curiosity seekers (not to mention the potential stalker), temperamental competitors, constant travel, and strange hotel suites. She was expected to fulfill ever-more-demanding public-relations responsibilities arising from her fast-rising position in the skating world. And all the while she was never allowed to neglect her training regimen, taking care to get the proper rest and diet.

As Sonja Henie once observed, "No one can warn or prepare you for the drawbacks of being constantly in the spotlight."

CHAPTER FOURTEEN

A Dream Realized

The caravan moved on to Edmonton, Canada. "The Gateway of the North," it was the site of the 1996 World Championships.

So far, Michelle had been able to approach each competition with the attitude, "you're competing against yourself." Not about the rivals she'd defeated, and those she hadn't, not about what their placements were.

She also thought about how she performed in practice every day; although this was Worlds, it should be no different for her than at practice. Everything would be fine if she could simply skate the way she did in practice.

Tara Lipinski was delighted to discuss how she'd skated at Nationals a few weeks earlier. "I skated one of the best programs in my life, and I was really happy," she said. "It felt just great."

Was she intimidated now by her first world competition? "It's even better than Nationals," she said, delighted to be with "all these world-class skaters." She said that she liked the attention, liked doing interviews.

The media loved Lipinski, reporting that she was nicknamed the "Boss" because "she knows what she wants."

Her diminutive size invited comparisons to Shirley Temple. She said she found it amazing, "really neat," to be on the same practice ice as Midori Ito, her idol.

Michelle's advice for Tara: have fun. She knew Lipinski had been training hard and was ready, so Tara should "just go for it."

When Carol Heiss, Tonia Kwiatkowski's coach, was thirteen years old and America's rising young skating prodigy, she competed in her first Worlds, which took place in Davos, Switzerland. She'd been so thrilled to be in Europe, to be competing in this prestigious event, that after the plane landed at the Swiss airport, she went outside and kissed the ground!

In her view, Kwan, Lipinski, and the others were not too young—and Kwiatkowski not too old—for all that was happening for them, although she felt that if one wanted to be the best, "do it for yourself, not for all the millions of dollars you can earn." But if a thirteen-, fourteen-, or fifteen-year-old—or a twenty-four-year-old, for that matter—could do the job, what did age matter? "Why not?" asked Heiss.

Tara held a similar view. "If the judges feel you're ready, you're ready."

Certainly Chen-Lu *was* ready. The defending world champion was in top form, beautiful to look at in the short program in her flowing gray, black, and rhinestone-studded costume. She skated to music appropriately titled "Spring Breeze."

From her performance, it would have been impossible to guess that in the not-too-distant past she'd had to overcome a foot injury serious enough to have doctors fearing permanent damage.

Her jumps were unusual, with her breathtaking ability to "delay" the triple rotations for a fraction of a second as she seemed to hover momentarily in the air. Her spins, though, were her weakest element, but the total package was impressive. As Richard Callaghan and many others have observed, "We've been told over and over the complete package wins."

A standing ovation from the crowd, plus technical scores ranging from 5.4 to 5.8, and presentation scores of 5.7 to 5.9, left room for others, but Lulu would be hard to beat.

Tara was perceived in a different light than the "serious contenders." She was here for the first time, to be appreciated for her precociousness and her promise, and to gain experience for the years ahead.

Skimming swiftly across the ice in her short program—she was skating to the overture from Leonard Bernstein's *On the Town*—she had a very difficult combination planned for the opening—a triple-lutz-double-loop combination (not a toe loop, which was easier). But she fell on the landing of the lutz, then fell again a moment later on a triple flip.

The audience supported her by hand-clapping in rhythm to subsequent sections of her music, and she completed her program powerfully. Her scores, however, had to have come as a shock: 3.8 to 4.6 for technical merit, 4.5 to 5.2 for presentation. She'd wind up in twenty-third place.

After this setback, Lipinski did not burst into tears or babble incoherently in kiss-and-cry; she retained her composure, although she was undoubtedly surprised: these had been the first mistakes she'd made all week.

Tara later admitted she'd allowed herself to become overconfident in the short when she saw that others, including Midori Ito, were doing poorly. She paid the price. It was a mistake she vowed never to repeat.

"I am still good," she said, "just had a bad day." Todd Eldredge's advice to her on the upcoming long program was succinct. "Just do it," he told her.

Was it possible for Kwan to surpass Chen-Lu?

When Michelle took to the ice for her short, the crowd grew silent. In her red costume, sparkling with black sequins, a red flower in her upswept hair, she looked enchanting. With her superb opening steps, she conveyed great emotion, interpreting the music with subtle but powerful grace. The cross-country tour she'd undertaken the year before had obviously enriched her ability to communicate with an audience.

She was so pleased afterward that when she left the ice and had hugged an elated Frank Carroll, she almost forgot to continue on to kiss-and-cry, confirming that in her own mind she'd competed with herself, won, and won the hearts of the audience.

For Michelle, that was enough.

Her scores for technical merit ranged from 5.6 to 5.9; for presentation, seven of the judges awarded her 5.9, the remaining two 5.8.

It wasn't such a good night for others. The reason for Frank Carroll's stubborn insistence that Michelle never become known for any particular jump or spin became painfully evident less than a minute into Midori Ito's program. Ito was famous for the triple axel, and on this night, skating to Stravinsky's *Firebird*, she began the preparation, soared high into the air, her tight body position exactly correct . . . then inexplicably fell out of the jump, landing on two feet.

It was all downhill from there. Ito seemed deflated as she sat unhappily in kiss-and-cry afterward, waiting for the disappointing scores: 5.2 to 5.4 for technical merit, 5.4 to 5.7 for presentation.

Meanwhile, Surya Bonaly took a disastrous fall on her triple lutz and wound up in seventh place going into the long.

Seventeen-year-old European champion Irina Slutskaya, wearing black and pink and looking like a thirteen-year-old, skated to a Latin beat and delivered the required elements well, although one didn't have to be a judge to observe that Tonia Kwiatkowski (who wound up ninth after the short) had outskated her.

Slutskaya, however, was the new European champion and hope for the future; her efforts brought technical scores of 5.6 to 5.8, artistic scores of 5.5 to 5.8.

After the short, Kwan was in first place, Chen-Lu second, Slutskaya third.

"Any skater dreams of being the world champion. It would be a dream come true," Michelle had said.

The skating order for the long program had Kwan in the final group of competitors, in the next-to-last spot; there'd be plenty of time to "think too much," if she permitted this to happen.

Irina Slutskaya would skate first, followed by Chen-Lu, Midori Ito, German champion Tanja Szewczenko, Kwan, and Russia's Maria Butyrskaya.

With the other competitors not in the final group, Surya Bonaly had been practicing a quadruple (*four* turns in the air) salchow, and hoped to unleash it in her long program. It never materialized, however, and she made many errors, at one point seeming to rearrange the elements in her program as she went along.

Tara Lipinski, however, brought down the house. There were no mistakes tonight. She presented an undeniably charismatic package, and moved up in the standings to a final fifteenth place.

Irina Slutskaya, skating to orchestral versions of the American musicals *They're Playing Our Song*, *A Chorus Line*, and songs of Jerome Kern, performed the long program with sustained speed but took a bad fall on her opening triple lutz, landed her second triple lutz poorly, wasn't in control of her spins at all times, and rarely pointed her toes! Her musical interpretation, at best, was arguably adequate.

Still, the judges loved her. She'd been the first Russian to become European champion and was full of energy and enthusiasm. If America had Michelle Kwan and now Tara Lipinski, Europe had Irina Slutskaya. They awarded her 5.7 to 5.8 for technical merit, 5.6 to 5.8 for presentation.

Chen-Lu, skating to Rachmaninoff's haunting Piano Concerto No.2, was in peak form. Sandra Bezic had done a superb job choreographing both of her programs, and the flow of the skater's movements was in perfect emotional harmony with the music.

The reigning world champion delivered a performance of Gold Medal caliber, and the judges acknowledged it:

5.8 to 5.9 for technical merit, and then . . . 5.8 up to two perfect 6.0s for artistic presentation.

The crowd roared its agreement.

As applause for Chen-Lu reverberated through the arena, Midori Ito, standing on the sidelines, ready but not eager to go on, made a poignant gesture of hope as she touched her coach's hand. Ito had seemed on the verge of becoming ill during warm-up.

This was to have been her triumphant return to the ranks of Olympic-division competition. She'd lost weight, made cosmetic improvements, and looked lovely in a lavender-and-white costume.

But nothing worked, not the way it should have. The pressure of competing seemed to have overwhelmed the petite athlete, and it seemed unlikely that the young woman who'd been an idol for so many, including Kwan and Lipinski, could or would want to remain "eligible" to compete in the '98 Olympics. Subsequently, it was reported that she was suffering from anemia.

Standing backstage in a windbreaker jacket, Chen-Lu watched and waited. She was in first place so far, and with those two perfect 6.0s, it seemed that she would win.

She said she felt very happy and confident, joyful in fact, but couldn't find the proper words in English to express her feelings.

Suspense mounted as the crowd grew impatient. Tanya Szewczenko, skating to music from the London and Broadway musical *Miss Saigon*, performed a well-received program, but everyone was waiting for Michelle to appear. If she came through, she'd be the third

youngest lady—behind Sonja Henie and Oksana Baiul—
ever to win the World Championship.

This was the moment.

For this performance, Michelle didn't skate the role of
Salome; she *lived* it. It was there inside her, stored up and
waiting to be turned loose. Skating is an art when it is
made an art . . . and that is what Kwan accomplished on
this evening.

She paced herself perfectly, letting "air" in at certain
moments to enable the audience to savor key movements. At one point she had to do some fast thinking,
because when her triple triple-toe-loop combination (the
only one in the competition) came up, she did a triple-
double combination instead.

Immediately the contingency plan clicked into gear:
instead of a double axel at the end, she'd have to put in a
triple toe, always a difficult move but even more so at
such a moment, since she'd be exhausted.

*It was very hard for me, after all those great skaters. . . .
I was near the end. . . . I had to put it all on the line. . . .*

The moment came. Not only was the jump performed,
it was completed *powerfully*, with spring, height, and
perfect form in the air and on the landing. A blockbuster
last impression to leave with the judges.

A roar of approval boomed from the audience; Michelle
seemed in a daze. She'd been mentally prepared for her
performance, but nothing could have prepared her for the
excitement she felt when it was over.

"I'm speechless," she finally said.

Could she have skated any better? She didn't think so.
"Everything went well tonight. I thank God for it."

*   *   *

Backstage, Chen-Lu appeared tense and anxious.

In kiss-and-cry, Michelle and Frank Carroll waited. Then: three 5.8s, six 5.9s for technical merit; seven 5.9s and *two perfect 6.0s* for presentation. Kwan and Carroll were incredulous. The final results: six judges had placed Kwan first. Chen-Lu had received only three first places.

A moment fraught with emotion for Chen-Lu, who was understandably crestfallen.

Michelle Kwan's face radiated joy. She was the youngest American ever to win the World Championship. "I'm very happy," she said tearfully, thanking friends, family, "and all who support me."

It had been an outstanding and meaningful victory. The defending champion had been brilliant, made no mistakes. If one was to express an opinion on what made the difference, perhaps it was Michelle's spins, which were far superior—better form, faster, more varied, and infinitely more refined. Both skaters had presented a complete package, but Kwan's was that extra little bit *more* complete.

"I thought both girls deserved to win," said Irina Slutskaya.

Michelle had once been asked if she thought of herself as fire or ice. Her reply: *"The wind*—I'm just gliding over the ice, watching everyone skating, seeing the crowd. I'm just flying everywhere. . . ."

She had indeed been born to skate. She'd had "a goal since I was born" . . . winning the World Championship.

Now she'd achieved that goal.

CHAPTER FIFTEEN

"I Can't Believe It!"

"I'm a world champion; I can't believe it!" Michelle exclaimed. "It has not really gone to my brain yet." At first she slept with her Gold Medal, but then, as she said, "It was, like, 'I won, get on with life.' "

Had she been nervous? "Not at all," she insisted. "I was so concentrated. Nothing could interfere. I knew the whole way through, 'Yeah, I'm going to kick some butt.' There was no doubt in my mind I could do it."

"I could see fire in her face," said Toller Cranston, who'd been on site for the competition. "In spite of the hair and the fancy clothes, she's a tough, little, feisty competitor. She's got spirit." Cranston found her respect for and devotion to Frank Carroll a major element of her success. She'd had no other primary coach. "That kind of loyalty brings success," he stated.

Danny Kwan was determined to keep his daughter on an even keel. *Of course* she must continue to work to improve even further, for if she learned to be satisfied, "it puts you at ease and you avoid the highs and lows."

There were no "lows" on the immediate horizon.

Frank Carroll had done it; he'd successfully engineered a skating-world coup. He acknowledged that one had to be a great athlete to become world champion, but athleticism was hardly enough. "If you don't have the look, the choreography, the music, it's impossible."

He admitted that there had been some adverse reaction to Michelle's "Salome." Letters had arrived saying it was "a sexist portrayal, or asking why you have a sweet, young girl portraying the violation of women," recalled Carroll. "It was crazy out there," he said, adding: "I don't understand."

It was an exciting period of adjustment for Michelle as she reaped the emotional and financial rewards of her victory (a fifty-city tour would reportedly earn her $750,000). But caution had not been thrown to the winds. Her agent, Shep Goldberg, expressed that protecting Michelle's future interests was a vital concern. "Money is not an exception to that rule. Michelle is selective in what she does. She turns down seventy-five percent of the requests she gets." Touring the country coast to coast and beyond, Michelle skated with heart and soul and audiences responded in kind.

In Alaska, on a fishing jaunt, she experienced the thrill of reeling in, by herself, a twenty-five-pound salmon. But while a thrashing fish, or a triple lutz, might not prove to be a problem for Michelle, the automobile did. She initially failed the three-point turn on her driver's test, but practice paid off and she passed the test in the summer of 1996.

Her father made certain Michelle didn't take her stardom for granted. When she asked him what, at this point, her weaknesses were and how she might overcome them, he offered two suggestions. One, appreciate your success. Two, appreciate your audiences.

One day on tour, en route to the bus, Michelle chose to avoid autograph seekers. Danny Kwan admonished her; one *should* sign autographs, he told her, explaining that all that Michelle now had came from the fans and she had to "learn to give back."

CHAPTER SIXTEEN

Sudden Fears

Frank Carroll had delivered an eerily prophetic statement after Michelle had won Worlds: "The way things are going, no one is going to be on top year after year. We just have to accept that."

Michelle was still working on her triple axel; she wanted it for '98. In the meantime, for the 1996–1997 season, the question was how could she top "Salome"? Where would the inspiration come from for an equally dramatic and effective concept?

For her new short program, William Shakespeare's great tragedy *Othello* ignited sparks. Michelle's character would be Desdemona, the gentle, innocent wife of the Moorish general Othello. In the play, Desdemona is murdered by her jealous husband, who accuses her of infidelity, ignoring her truthful pleas of innocence. Othello, who "loved not wisely, but too well," then kills himself.

Michelle's long program was based on a legend. Everyone knew of the mysteriously beautiful Taj Mahal, the marble tomb in India that stands in a garden containing pools that reflect its glory. Over the years millions of people have visited the monument and gazed awe-struck at the sight.

Yet how many are aware of its history?

Three hundred years ago, the ruler Shah Jahan ordered it built in memory of his favorite wife. Her title, Mumtaz-i-Mahal, which means "pride of the palace," gave the building its name. The bodies of the Shah and his wife lie in a vault below the splendid structure.

The romantic love the Shah felt for his late wife was the inspiration for many love stories. Indeed, at one point, actress Vivien Leigh, famous for her portrayal of Scarlett O'Hara in *Gone With the Wind*, was to play the Mumtaz-i-Mahal, but the film never materialized.

It was decided that Michelle Kwan would "portray" the wife in her long program.

As the January date for Nationals approached, the butterflies in Michelle's stomach seemed to have taken up permanent residence. *Why couldn't she relax?* She was world champion, and she always delivered the goods.

"Everybody says, 'You're on a roll,' " she said, laughing. "It doesn't feel like it."

In the theater, there is a saying that success is a problem more difficult than failure. Apparently, Michelle was experiencing some of the problems attendant on success.

This was the first time she was defending champion. The pressure of being number one is unrelenting. Anyone who's been there has had trouble adjusting—whether it be in the world of sports, motion pictures, theater, music, literature, politics. . . . You can't "train" for it; there are no courses to teach you how to handle being a world champion of anything. "Any true warrior—any true competitor will not entertain the idea of losing," observed film director Spike Lee about top-of-the-line athletes.

"When you're defending, you're always looking behind, over your shoulder," explained Frank Carroll. Interestingly, his view on the subject echoed Spike Lee's: "I tell Michelle, 'This is war, you're a soldier out there to do battle and not to second-guess yourself.' " He was trying to encourage Michelle to skate "and not to think too much"; to prevent her from dwelling on questions that could only debilitate her, questions like, "If I don't skate well, will I still go to the Olympics?"

Carroll's belief in his student's talent went beyond her simply winning another title. He considered her capable "of becoming one of the great skaters of all time with her ability to perform extraordinarily dramatic portrayals." Few were capable of it. "They just skate to pretty music. There's more to Michelle than just pretty."

Michelle had taken time off, bowed out of a few events, to concentrate on the new routines. Sister Karen, attending Boston University as a freshman, wanted her to take a break and visit her for a week, but Michelle opted to continue her training, and even bypassed skating several exhibitions in Japan, which would have earned her a great deal of money.

World champion Todd Eldredge had learned the hard way that being on the road was not conducive to good training. "It's hard to improve while traveling." Losing the national title last year to Rudy Galindo "probably made me a little more aware of the need to get home and get training and get into shape."

Another problem Kwan faced: breaking in new boots.

This proved to be more than a minor annoyance; the perfect fit and feel of one's boots is absolutely essential to a good performance. The last thing on any skater's mind should be a problem with her boots! One had to make certain they didn't squeeze the foot or put pressure on points where pressure oughtn't to be.

Placement of the blades on the soles of the boot, finding that exact "right spot," can be an excruciatingly delicate procedure. If the blades are screwed in a fraction of an inch in the wrong position, one's balance is off, takeoffs on jumps won't "feel" right, and spins won't be centered.

Competitions have been lost because of "new" boots. Canadian pairs champions Barbara Underhill and Paul Martini, the favorites going into the '84 Olympics, literally fell out of the running because Barbara's new boots hadn't been properly broken in!

For the '84 Worlds the following month, Barbara wore her old boots and the pair easily won the title.

Like any other teenager, Kwan was interested in what headline makers in other fields were up to. She liked Harrison Ford and Julia Roberts. The Clint Eastwood thriller about a Secret Service man, *In the Line of Fire*, captured her imagination. She had been deeply moved by *Night*, the Elie Wiesel book about the Holocaust. She loved listening to Elvis Presley CDs, and Bette Midler was another favorite. When not in training, she enjoyed playing basketball, although she considered herself a poor player. She loved to swim, and enjoyed visiting local amusement parks.

"Oh my God, Brad Pitt got engaged!" she exclaimed on hearing the news that the actor and Gwyneth Paltrow had become affianced. "How could he do this to me? I'm doomed. I bet everyone is crying."

"Not everyone," quipped Danny Kwan.

(Michelle's and others "worries" on this score proved short-lived; by June 1997, it was announced that Pitt's engagement was off.)

Michelle loved to shop, and with her income reportedly slated to climb this year up to $1 million, she could afford to be indulgent. She had bought herself a pair of diamond earrings, as a reward for winning Worlds.

Chanel was a favorite designer, but the young skater resisted the impulse to splurge. "I still don't want to spend ten thousand dollars on a suit."

Michelle carried no credit cards. "Can't trust her," joked her dad.

Her favorite outfit was a T-shirt and jeans, black and turquoise her preferred colors.

As far as Frank Carroll was concerned, Michelle would come through the upcoming competitive season with flying colors. He compared her with a previous star pupil, former world champion Linda Fratianne. "There are tremendous similarities with work habits, dedication, consistency, cooperation, an inner strength which really can't be taught. They both look like little flowers, but inside there's a core of metal, a strength that's unbelievable."

Michelle was determined to believe that.

Michelle was under no illusions that because she was world champion, everybody adored her. Being on top of the mountain placed her "in the bull's-eye. I'm trying to move away so no one will shoot me!" she said, explaining that she was trying to focus on her skating and not worry about competitors, because the only one who could defeat her was herself—or as contemporary philosopher Deepak Chopra phrased the dilemma: "My tormentor is myself left over from yesterday."

With sister Karen, who was no longer training full-time, Michelle traveled to Paris, where they competed in the Trophée Lalique competition. Michelle's boots continued to require adjustments. However, she won the short program hands down. "Desdemona" turned out to be a masterpiece, delivered by a master. The routine included a sweeping inside-edge spiral, twice as difficult as one on the outside edge, and Michelle delivered it with a deep lean, great speed, gorgeous extension, and complete control. This move alone placed her far above others in style.

Her long program was memorable as well. She had problems on her double axel and triple flip (her boots were bothering her), but she didn't stumble or fall. "Tilted" in the air on these jumps, she managed to land them correctly. Skaters who are able to "rescue" jumps this way are said to have "cat feet," and Michelle was definitely one of these skaters.

Her final spin sequence was a knockout—various spins in different positions, all emanating from the initial spin. All positions were impeccable.

She won the event. Russia's Maria Butyrskaya, an attractive young woman who always managed to finish near the top despite stylistic shortcomings, won second place. Tara Lipinski finished third; Karen Kwan, seventh.

There was virtually no doubt in anyone's mind that Michelle would triumph in the 1997 U.S. Nationals in February, then the final Skate America challenge in

Canada, followed by the World Championships in Lausanne in March.

During the year Kwan lost a dear friend, Harris Collins, a producer of the Tour of World Figure Skating Champions, who had died rinkside. She expressed her grief and her respect for Collins the best way she knew how: she created an exhibition program dedicated to him. She wore white, skated to music called "Winter," and performed with heartfelt emotion that was communicated to her audience. It was a tribute, all agreed, that Collins would have loved.

Meanwhile, demons of doubt were plaguing another skater, also a friend of Michelle's. On Sunday, January 12, 1997, at 2:30 A.M., a green Mercedes-Benz sedan was speeding down a country road in Simsbury, Connecticut. The sound of screeching brakes suddenly broke the silence as the automobile veered out of control, hurtled off the road, and smashed into dense shrubbery.

Based on the skid marks on the road, police reports later estimated the speed of the vehicle at ninety-seven miles per hour. It was a miracle the passengers weren't killed.

The driver turned out to be a former Olympic and world champion whose balletic style had exerted a major influence on Kwan's skating and who had helped Michelle create her makeup for "Salome."

But of late, Oksana Baiul had not been focusing her energies on the ice; she'd been pursuing other interests. These were reported to include parties, shopping, cooking Russian food, watching *Melrose Place*, experimenting with makeup, and cheering on the Hartford Whalers.

She'd been having back problems, said to be a residual

effect of the on-ice collision back in '94, and had put on weight (her body was still maturing). She'd bleached her hair blond.

On that chilly January 12 evening, the Mercedes was totaled. A concussion and scalp wound were the extent of Oksana's injuries, but her dark-haired, dark-eyed companion in the automobile, thirty-year-old professional figure skater Ararat ("Ari") Zakarian, might have been killed. Fortunately, he escaped with no more than a broken finger.

Zakarian pulled the unconscious Oksana from the car. He later revealed to *International Figure Skating* magazine that the skater had tried to avoid running over an animal on the road, and that she had been excited at hearing a Madonna song on the radio. Everything had happened very fast.

Baiul's arrest on January 14—she turned herself in voluntarily—coincided with a statement from Tonya Harding that she intended to return to skating the following month in an exhibition in Reno, Nevada.

Oksana was charged with driving under the influence—her blood alcohol content registered at .168, way above the .10 limit—and with reckless driving. The legal drinking age in Connecticut is twenty-one. Oksana was nineteen at the time of the accident.

Surrounded by a phalanx of photographers and cameramen who were waiting for her outside the courtroom, a very pale and shaken-up Baiul disappeared inside the building. She promised the judge she would appear at a hearing on January 27 and was released.

Her lawyer, Daniel Blume, said that she understood the seriousness of the matter and acknowledged putting herself and others in danger. "She knows she sent the wrong message to millions of her fans around the world."

Here was a lesson in pitfalls to be avoided by one who wins figure-skating Gold. All who knew Oksana—and the Kwans were certainly among them—were concerned but not shocked. After turning professional, Oksana had seemed to lose her competitive spirit, and she'd recently pulled out of several professional competitions.

"I get the feeling now she doesn't want to be skating," said Brian Boitano. "When you reach a huge goal, sometimes you say, 'Okay, now I want to do something different.' " Boitano said he'd felt young at twenty-four when he won the '88 Olympics. "I can't imagine winning at sixteen," he said. "You turn into a celebrity overnight. It alters your life and takes years to adjust to."

Baiul's hairstylist, Johnny LaVoie, was quoted as saying that Oksana "is not the monster she is portrayed to be. People need to have a childhood. She hasn't had one."

David Letterman, in one of his TV monologues, observed how Oksana had lost control of her car, was arrested for drunk driving, and "according to police reports, her blood alcohol level was .16, .16, .15, .16, .16, .16, .15, and .14 from the East German judge."

But Carol Heiss Jenkins wasn't joking about the skater's predicament when she said: "Everyone in the skating world saw something was going to happen with Oksana. I certainly am not blaming her. We all have to be aware in our sport [that] with all the newfound fame and wealth, we have to give these young champions guidance."

* * *

Ironically, Baiul supposedly had the right people to give her guidance. Her problem had to do with how much she was listening to them.

Oksana issued a statement declaring that she was very sorry for the mistake she made, and she apologized to "the many people who have supported me in the past, and I ask for their understanding."

Ekaterina Gordeyeva understood: "Everything came too fast for her," she said. "I think maybe she didn't know how to handle it—all the money and success." The figure-skating community was a close-knit group, and Gordeyeva spoke for all of Oksana's friends, Michelle included, when she declared: "We are all here to help her."

The contrast between Oksana Baiul and Michelle Kwan was not overlooked by those close to Baiul. "I look at Michelle Kwan, all the success she has had as a teenager, her great image; her family does a lot for her," observed Nina Petrenko, daughter of Baiul's coach, and wife of former Olympic champion Viktor Petrenko.

Michelle's family was there for her, but they couldn't skate for her. That was her job, and she believed she was focused on it to the best of her ability. "Train hard, be happy, and don't worry about anything," had been her advice to budding young skaters several seasons back.

A lot had happened since then.

CHAPTER SEVENTEEN

~~

A Very Tough Season

In the sport of mountain climbing, there is a saying: "Those who scale Mt. Everest have to be prepared for a systems breakdown."

As February 1997 and the start of Nationals drew close, Frank Carroll reflected on Michelle's position in the scheme of things. "I don't feel she's been challenged a lot," he said. "But somewhere along the line there's a little girl coming up, and she's going to be damn good and give [Michelle] a run for her money. That's healthy. That's life. That's sport. I don't see that right now. But it will come. It always does."

It must have been a daunting responsibility, trying to be the "Michelle Kwan" everyone was writing about. While Michelle seemed able to face the challenge, she later admitted, "It was a dreadful time for me. [Going into Nationals] seemed like I had something to lose—more to lose than to gain." Apparently Michelle herself wasn't reflecting on the lack of challenge in her life; she was concerned with defending the title, living up to the media's (and everyone else's) image of her as the most artistic, consistent figure skater of the day. The best of the best, perfect all the time. Meanwhile, there were photo shoots, social engagements, interviews.

Michelle commented that if one is feeling pressured, it comes from within. "You have to enjoy everything you do!" Skating was only a sport, a hobby; she had a "goofy, silly" side to her, too, though it didn't interfere with the hardworking skater. "I'm not an alien or a super-duper jumping machine who lands on her feet all the time," she said. "I'm normal!"

Michelle's port in a storm was her family. "We always talk about life and what's going through my head; we don't hide anything. Oh God, it would be a lonely world if I didn't have my family. They're so much a part of me."

Karen was scheduled to compete at Nationals once again, and the sisters would have each other to confide in. For Michelle, her family was "the secret ingredient. Without them, I'd be nothing. I always want to be 'Michelle,' well-grounded."

The U.S. Nationals were to be held in Nashville, Tennessee, home of country music. The cream of the nation's crop of skaters gathered there to compete.

"Each competition is a battle," Carroll, always honest and straightforward, told Michelle. "I told her to go out and be a fighter. Don't fight to defend the castle, fight to take the castle. Skate to win; don't skate not to lose. It's different when you're defending a title for the first time."

Oftentimes trying too hard to make something happen results in a negative outcome.

"I put myself in a state," recalled Michelle about her attitude before this competition. She'd felt tense, not really herself. She tried to tell herself that this was just another competition, she was here to have fun. But somehow fun was absent from the agenda.

"It didn't feel like I was ready," she said in retrospect. "Physically, yes. But my mind was smoking, it was on fire. I really couldn't put it out at that point."

She experienced a further realization: "If this is pressure," she asked herself, whether or not it was self-inflicted, "what is next year going to be like?"

"It can be literally terrifying, the enormity of skating in front of all those people and on television," observed Brian Boitano's coach, Linda Leaver.

Frank Carroll had cautioned Michelle about skating too conservatively. Her body was changing. "Going through puberty on national television is hard," noted Christy Ness, Kristi Yamaguchi's coach.

"It's easier when you don't have a [curvaceous] body," said Tonia Kwiatkowski's choreographer, Glynn Watts.

Word was spreading that Michelle was under a lot of stress. "She'll be okay," said those in the know.

Yet in practice, Michelle was suddenly having big trouble with her jumps. This was unusual for the skater who, beginning with Worlds last year, had won Gold in all but one of the dozen Olympic-style events she'd competed in.

She not only had trouble in practice, but the fates weren't working for her on other fronts. While the senior division contained twenty competitors, she was slated to be the second to skate the short program.

This was a strange and unexpected development— although the luck of the draw. Michelle had grown accustomed to performing well into the evening, when the arena was full, the judges and the audience settled in.

After all, she was the defending champion. To have her present her short program at the top of the evening was equivalent to having the main group at a rock concert perform before the warm-up band.

"It was awkward. It didn't feel like a competition to me," Kwan said afterward. "It happened so quickly, boom, I was done. I didn't see any cameras in my face, I was like: 'Where is everybody? I'm here!' "

Nevertheless, Michelle got through it and won the short program. Tara Lipinski was in second place; her coach had told her not even to think about winning, and she followed his advice. Her goal was simply to make the world team.

Tonia Kwiatkowski was in third after the short, and Nicole Bobek, having missed on major elements, was in sixth place. Karen Kwan also performed well, her triple-toe-double-toe combination textbook perfect.

Carlo Fassi, now Nicole Bobek's coach—along with Carlo's wife, Christa, they were training at Michelle's haunt, Lake Arrowhead—looked over the rest of the field and had this to say: "Presentation is what's missing in skating. Thirteen- and fourteen-year-old girls jump beautifully, but they are only jumping. You are a little kid, not a woman."

He wasn't referring to Michelle, Nicole, Tonia Kwiatkowski, or Karen Kwan, but as for the rest of the competitors . . .

Fassi's observations carried weight; one of the legends of figure skating, the sixty-seven-year-old veteran of countless ice wars had been inducted into the United States Figure Skating Association (USFSA) Hall of Fame in 1994 (Frank Carroll had been awarded that honor in '96). He'd participated as coach or athlete in all Olympic Winter Games from 1948 to 1992. Peggy Fleming, John

Curry, Dorothy Hamill, and Robin Cousins, Olympic and world champions all, had been his pupils, as was later world champion Jill Trenary.

But while a coach can do his best to encourage and motivate, it is up to the student to find his or her own center of comfort. Nicole Bobek, for one, was still searching.

One lesson was that it was virtually impossible to please the media for long. Bobek had lost sixteen pounds, but now the press speculated: "Is she *too* thin?" In practice here in Nashville, her jumps were great but hardly made reporters forget that she'd had back problems and hadn't done well in a recent competition.

Sonja Henie had summed it up perfectly decades earlier: "You have to shut everything out of your mind when you're out there except what you have to do. Once other thoughts barge in, you're in trouble."

Trouble was in store for several of the top skaters this season. Last year's pair champions, Jenni Meno and Todd Sand, whose marriage Michelle had attended in Cleveland, suffered a disastrous short program. Sand's concentration had faltered on a key lift, there was a fall, and the couple also fell out of tempo with their music. The two skaters were shocked, but said they were relieved it happened here and not at next month's Worlds.

They fared better, but made mistakes, on the long program, and there was an upset: pairs team Jason Dungjen and Kyoko Ino, who'd placed second for the past three seasons, seized the moment. They took nothing for granted; every moment on the ice they concentrated intently on their skating. They won the competition, with Meno and Sand placing second.

* * *

When Nicole Bobek, lovely as always, skated out onto the ice for her long program in sparkling red and white, she seemed to have little chance of winning. Her poor showing in the short had confirmed the doubts of the skeptics.

Skating to the classic *Giselle*, she opened the long program with a spectacular double axel and went on from there, integrating a superior triple-lutz-double-toe-loop combination, a triple salchow, her terrific spiral sequence, and a series of other jumps and spins into an exciting choreographic pattern.

She was *on* tonight, everything was working, and by the time she'd finished, the audience was on its feet. In the stands, her mother's face expressed both joy and relief.

The old adage had once again proven to be true: *expect the unexpected, especially in figure skating.* Nicole won 5.4 to 5.8 for technical merit, 5.6 to 5.8 for presentation. Suddenly she'd once again become a contender.

Tonia Kwiatkowski had worked hard this season on making her program "mean something." She was doing the same in her personal life, and had playfully expressed her displeasure at always being identified as the "oldest competitor" (she was now twenty-six). So what? she wanted to know. "What difference does it make?"

Skating to the "Hungarian Rhapsody," she got off to a good start until the all-important triple lutz, when she took a bad spill. Things didn't improve from there, and her technical marks, 4.9 to 5.4, and presentation scores, 4.8 to 5.7, eliminated any chance at Gold or Silver.

Because Tonia had been in third place in the short, and

Bobek in sixth, it seemed momentarily possible that Kwiatkowski might hang on to third.

Then a young teenager named Angela Nikodinov shattered Kwiatkowski's chances by delivering the goods, winning 5.5 to 5.8 for technical, 5.4 to 5.8 for presentation.

With Michelle and Tara left to skate, the scores were tabulated and Nicole Bobek was in first place, Nikodinov second, and Kwiatkowski third.

Michelle looked sober on the sidelines as Frank Carroll spoke intently to her at rinkside. Still, she was beautiful to look at, every inch the princess she was portraying in her glistening red-and-gold costume, her hair gathered into a bun, her face beautifully made up, a sequin in the middle of her forehead.

"Ladies and gentlemen . . . Michelle Kwan . . ."

The crowd hushed. She assumed her opening stance. The music began, and her opening choreography was exquisite, delicately graceful, performed with confidence and power. A perfectly controlled flying camel spin flowed into the preparatory steps for the crucial triple-lutz-double-toe combination.

Yes!

Next came the triple triple-toe-loop combination . . . *and then it happened.*

On the landing of the second jump, which had turned into a double toe, she appeared to slip—in fact, she'd landed on the flat of her blade—not the toe pick and the back outside edge, as she was supposed to—and her free leg swung wide. She hadn't checked out of the jump forcefully enough. It had all happened in a split second; she lost her balance and fell, hard, turning over onto her stomach.

Total shock engulfed all viewers.

"It wasn't so much the pressure," Michelle later recalled. "I was more frightened after I stumbled. I kind of panicked."

Everyone held their breath. In her next jump, the triple flip, she stumbled on the landing, although she didn't fall.

An excellent double axel and splendid footwork sequence followed, but her second triple lutz was aborted into a double.

"I wasn't concentrating enough. I guess I panicked in the middle of the performance after that fall. I got scared."

A smashing triple salchow, followed by a secure, high-in-the-air triple toe loop, a final back-bend position, and the program was over.

A nonplussed Michelle, pressing her hands to her cheeks in disbelief, acknowledged the ovation. "Thank you," she said, apologetic, almost embarrassed. She waved bravely to the audience.

Backstage, the concern on Karen Kwan's face was painfully apparent. One can only imagine how their mom and dad felt.

Michelle managed, just barely, to retain her composure in kiss-and-cry. Frank Carroll tried to comfort her as they waited for the scores: 5.3 to 5.7 for technical, 5.6 to 5.9 for presentation.

Despite her slipups, Michelle moved into first place, with Tara left to skate.

After Kwan's performance, the expression on Tara's face backstage said it all. Her coach, Richard Callaghan, spoke a few final words to her. She took to the ice, wearing white, her hair in a bun. She looked like a beautiful doll on the top of a wedding cake.

Skating to the movie soundtracks of *Sense and Sensibility* and *Much Ado About Nothing*, with a program choreographed by the highly experienced Sandra Bezic, she carefully seized the moment. She must not repeat last year's mistake at Worlds, where she'd become overconfident after others had erred.

Her technical elements—a triple flip, triple-lutz-double-toe-loop combination, and the most difficult version of the camel spin, performed on the flat of the blade—were performed flawlessly, as was her *pièce de résistance*, a triple-loop-triple-loop (not the less difficult toe loop) combination.

Incredible! True, the jumps didn't soar into the air and over the ice, but they were neat, clean, and complete.

If she didn't falter from this point on, the title was most likely hers. But she was courageous and daring, following through with a second triple lutz, a double-axel-triple-salchow combination, and a final triple toe.

The audience was on its feet.

"I'm so proud of you!" exclaimed coach Richard Callaghan as she stepped off the ice. She screamed out loud on seeing the marks: five 5.9s, four 5.8s for technical merit; three 5.9s, six 5.8s for presentation.

Overwhelmed, she gasped joyously for breath.

She'd won. Nicole Bobek hugged her as the ovation from the audience continued, so intensely that Tara had to walk back to the entrance to the ice and wave to the crowd.

Backstage, Frank Carroll fought to raise Michelle's spirits. She declined an interview with reporters.

* * *

A bubbly Nicole Bobek said that going into this competition, she hadn't wanted people to forget about her. In sixth place going into the long program, she had nothing to lose and had felt "really confident." Tonight's results were miraculous: she'd placed a final third, and thanked God and her support team. (Angela Nikodinov finished fourth, Tonia Kwiatkowski had slipped to sixth, and Karen Kwan finished in seventh place.)

Tara, too, had had nothing to lose; it was Michelle who'd had to endure the pressure of being the defending champion.

Lipinski was thrilled she'd brought off her triple-triple combination; she'd practiced hard, and "it was great when I landed it."

She felt confident she'd do better in Worlds this year than last year's fifteenth-place finish. She made the point that while she hadn't done her best in the short last year, she had showed the audience a good long program.

The Worlds would be in Lausanne, Switzerland, and Tara, the youngest U.S. Senior Ladies champion in the history of the sport, already had her passport.

At last, Michelle pulled herself together and faced the media. Her poor warm-up prior to skating the long program hadn't affected her at all, she said. Tonight she'd learned yet another lesson—to be able to step onto the podium and accept defeat (although hopefully Michelle derived some comfort from having received the Silver).

She wanted to thank the audience for helping her out, because in the middle of the program, when they started applauding, "It brought me back to life."

CHAPTER EIGHTEEN

~~

The Road Gets Rougher

Many thoughts, none of them positive, ran rampant in Michelle's brain in the aftermath of her title loss. "At Nationals, I wasn't fearless," she has recalled. "I was afraid of something." It was as though "at that point I was eaten by [a] monster."

She felt she'd been thinking all wrong, as though someone knew her inner competitive "secret code," and she was aware that permitting herself to have fearful thoughts was "so stupid!"

There was no consoling her. "If I had won, I would have felt equally bad," she said. "It would have been like, 'I skated terrible and I won? What's up with that?'"

Not that such a development was impossible. Peggy Fleming had won the '68 Olympics after a disappointing free-skating performance, including popping a planned double axel into a single and two-footing a landing on another key jump. Her concentration, like Michelle's, had vanished mid-program.

Frank Carroll was relieved that this wasn't an Olympic year. "Right now it's Michelle's battle against Michelle," he said, "and I guess she's fighting it out now instead of next year."

* * *

This phenomenon isn't restricted to figure skaters. When golfing champion Greg Norman suffered an equivalent disaster, his explanation said it all: "I choked," he said simply. Tension and nerves kicked in, leading him to add: "I'm my own worst enemy."

Norman explained he'd begun questioning himself, inflicted the damage himself, like a woodpecker constantly pecking away at himself. "I'm the only one who can screw up. I'm the only one that can make it happen," he said.

Michelle felt she'd expected too much of herself at Nashville, and perhaps had given herself "no options." "I didn't have the guts—and of course there was no glory!" The loss had been "a big downfall" for her, and she knew she had to get herself back together.

On a scale of one to ten, her confidence level had plummeted to "a one, almost a negative," she admitted.

She felt she'd performed like "a chicken with its head cut off," like "a little kitty being eaten by a wolf." She recalled she "kind of went loony . . . and that's the worst thing you can do."

She was determined to avoid a repeat performance.

As far as the public was concerned, Frank Carroll was unruffled by Michelle's dilemma. Losing to Tara wasn't a catastrophe, he said; things happened in life, in sport. Kwan was human, not some statue wearing a vine-leaf crown.

Privately, he was working hard to help her change her mental focus. The strategy was to have her get angry at herself, Carroll later revealed, and understand that potentially she was "capable of being in a class by herself."

* * *

Meanwhile, Tara's coach, Richard Callaghan, was too experienced and knowledgeable about the delicate balance that exists in figure skaters' psyches to appear overconfident about his protégée. He considered Tara intelligent enough to recognize that she had had a great night and the champion had had an off night. "Because she had a great night, she's the champion. But there are a lot of years left in her career, and there will be a lot of highs and lows."

Still, there was no question about it: Michelle now was vulnerable and others knew it. "It's like blood in the water in a tank of sharks," remarked observers, off the record but on the mark.

Frank Carroll focused on restoring Michelle's confidence; part of the process was to make her realize she was to skate her best *for herself*, not for her parents, friends, or anyone else. The Nationals, the Worlds—forget about them. This was exactly the advice Tiger Woods's dad offered his son before a major tournament: "Play [your game] with your mind. Play intelligently. Don't [defeat] yourself."

But the problem isn't so easily resolved, and Michelle would later compare her state of mind during this period to being in a coma. Entering the Champion Series Final in Hamilton, Ontario, she didn't mince words: she wanted to show everyone she still had it. "This is a fight, it's a war," she said.

She didn't want to deal with any negatives about her skating; having to see tapes of her mistakes at Nationals broadcast over and over was equivalent to listening to a broken record endlessly replayed.

Unfortunately, though, more frustration was in store as

she struggled again with her jumps. Of her short program at the Hamilton, Ontario, event, Michelle said, "Maybe I was waiting for that perfect takeoff [on the triple-lutz-double-toe combination] and I missed it. I couldn't hold on."

She didn't panic, however. This time she attacked the next jump without hesitation. "I have to go into the jumps with the eye of the tiger," she said.

Michelle wasn't the only champion in trouble. Todd Eldredge missed his triple axel, and said this mistake had just been plain "stupid." Jenni Meno and Todd Sand were also at a low ebb; they finished fourth out of four at this event.

Michelle won Silver. Tara Lipinski confounded the skeptics, did her job, and brought home Gold.

Switzerland. Located high in the snowcapped European Alps, its green valleys and blue lakes resemble a greeting-card painting come to life. Lausanne, a tourist center less than a mile from Lake Geneva, offers a breathtaking view of the lake and the mountains, and into this fairy-tale-like setting, only two weeks after the Champion Series Final, came Michelle Kwan, Tara Lipinski, Nicole Bobek, *et al.* Champions and their trainers from all over the world converged in the beautiful, picturesque city to make their dreams for 1997 World Championship Gold come true.

The media was ready for them.

Barely three days into the competition, ominous news swept through the skating community. Michelle was stunned to learn that her friend Scott Hamilton had been diagnosed with cancer. A legend to all skaters, Hamilton had overcome many obstacles, triumphing numerous times in the face of adversity. To Michelle, he had seemed indestructible.

His energy was the envy of skaters a dozen years his junior. To Michelle and others, Hamilton represented everything positive and inspiring about achieving and maintaining goals. He was both a mentor and big brother, a friend and confidant. He'd been a rock of Gibraltar to Ekaterina Gordeyeva after her husband Sergei's death.

Scott was very sensitive to the pressures and stress fellow skaters were subjected to, and they often turned to him for advice and encouragement. He felt the problems of success were hard enough to cope with when in one's twenties: "Can you imagine what it's like for a fourteen- or fifteen-year-old?" he observed.

He'd begun skating at age nine, considerably older than Michelle, Tara, Kristi, and most other champion-caliber skaters, although the men, in general, seemed to get a later start than the ladies. Figure skating had provided the physical therapy that turned the tide in Hamilton's battle with a potentially disabling childhood affliction, malabsorption syndrome.

Twenty-five years old when he'd won the Olympics in 1984, Hamilton was also a four-time World champion and winner of more pro-am events than any figure skater in history. Now thirty-eight, Hamilton had always seemed to be in supreme physical condition, but recently had been experiencing severe abdominal and lower-back pain while on tour with his show, Discover Stars on Ice.

After a recent show in East Lansing, Michigan, he was rushed to an emergency room. His subsequent decision, to go to the St. Francis Medical Center in Peoria, Illinois, for tests, had been kept secret. During a CAT scan, a tumor was discovered in his abdomen, and the subsequent diagnosis at the Cleveland Clinic Foundation, where Dr. Eric Klein, a urologist, and Dr. Ronald Bukowski, an oncologist, were on the case, was testicular cancer.

Fortunately—if such a word can be used—this is the most common and curable cancer in men between fifteen and forty, and Hamilton's prognosis was reportedly hopeful. The cure rate today is 80 to 90 percent, some said as high as 95 percent. Chemotherapy treatments would be necessary for a period of several months, and Hamilton would be treated as an outpatient.

Hamilton's friends were as shocked as he was. "Knowing Scott as well as I do," said lifelong friend Elaine Zayak, "he's always been a fighter. Everybody knows that, in the skating world especially." But his sense of humor hadn't deserted him. When informed by doctors of his condition, he said he was relieved it was nothing serious. When the doctors said it *was* serious, he had to explain that he understood that, he was only being funny!

Hamilton's official comment on his condition was not meant to be funny but was equally characteristic of the courageous skater. "With my own belief that the only disability in life is a bad attitude," he said, "I feel one hundred percent confident that I can overcome this disease and be back on the ice within a few months."

Within eight hours, another bombshell dropped. Carlo Fassi, here in Lausanne coaching, in addition to Nicole Bobek, a Romanian skater, Cornel Gheorghe, was working with Gheorghe on the Thursday morning preceding Friday's ladies' short program. Fassi complained of indigestion. Just before noon, he said he felt dizzy. Then he collapsed.

An ambulance was summoned to the Malley Sports Center, which rushed him to Canton Hospital–University Vaud. A man with no previous history of heart problems, Fassi suffered a massive heart attack and was pronounced dead at 2:30 P.M.

Nicole Bobek was devastated. She'd grown to love Fassi like a father, and felt she'd made it back to Worlds because of him. He'd protected her, helped her, and suddenly he was gone. Christa Fassi, Carlo's wife and fellow coach, told her that one of his last wishes was that she be with Nicole for the competition.

And so she was. After a sleepless night Bobek had an excellent warm-up the following afternoon, just prior to skating her short program. But when she looked over at Christa, she began to cry. "I know how hard it was on her," Nicole later said, "but it meant so much to have her with me."

Wearing a white costume trimmed in black and gold, Bobek looked beautiful. The audience, respectful and supportive, understood her plight. Her music began. She performed her opening steps and built up great speed, preparing for her combination, the triple-lutz-double-toe-loop. Her entrance and posture looked right, but she fell out of the jump, a major mandatory point deduction.

Her mother, in the stands, visibly blanched at the error, her hands shaking from nerves. Bobek managed a powerful double axel, but then fell on her triple toe.

Under the circumstances, her tears were understandable. Technical marks ranged from 4.6 to 5.0, presentation scores from 5.4 to 5.7.

* * *

Attention is always focused on the top competitors, but on very rare occasions a new face momentarily breaks through. Such was the case with eighteen-year-old Vanessa Gusmeroli, runner-up in the French Senior Ladies' championships and sixth in the European championships. There was polite applause now as she skated to center ice to begin her short program.

Performing to the soundtrack of the Jim Carrey film *The Mask*, Gusmeroli opened with a triple-loop-double-loop-jump combination, very difficult and very well done (Tara Lipinski's long program featured the triple-triple version of this same combination).

Unique combination spins and exciting choreography followed, and the spotlight of interest suddenly shone on this young woman. The judges acknowledged her expertise: 5.5 to 5.8 for technical merit, 5.7 to 5.8 for presentation.

Backstage, wearing green velvet with white lace trim, her hair in a ponytail, lipstick and mascara highlighting her features, Tara Lipinski was hopping from one foot to the other, like a boxer, as she listened to a pep talk from her coach, Richard Callaghan.

On the ice, performing to the soundtrack of the film *Little Women*, the petite skater proceeded to demonstrate her most powerful weapon to date: consistency. She'd packed her short program with a triple-lutz-double-loop combination, a triple flip, double axel, and spin combinations that were powerful, centered, and fast.

Slightly tilted in the air on the triple lutz, she had no trouble on the landing. Her choreography, by Sandra Bezic, took full advantage of the ice surface, and she displayed the mark of a true champion: control.

The judges rated her 5.5 to 5.8 for technical merit, 5.6 to 5.8 for presentation. Not unbeatable, by any means, but enough to move her into first place.

Russia's twenty-four-year-old Maria Butyrskaya, now a redhead, looked dramatic in a costume of green sequins. Her long legs gave her a striking silhouette on the ice, and she delivered a complex program that never for a moment seemed effortless.

The landings on her jumps weren't always secure, but she completed all the elements, looked good doing them, and the judges weren't unfriendly: 5.4 to 5.7 for technical merit, 5.4 to 5.8 for presentation.

Michelle, striking in a glittering black Versace costume, her hair gathered into a bun, appeared confident. She'd been telling herself that no one could beat her except herself; she knew that for sure. There was a somber but determined expression on her face while she stood with Frank Carroll at rinkside; then she smiled radiantly on skating to center ice.

"Dreams of Desdemona" began, and the flow of her movements, the power and extension on her spirals was wonderful to behold. She built up great speed, preparing for the all-important triple-lutz-double-toe-loop combination. She reached back with her free leg to tap into the ice and vault herself into the air . . . and fell out of the jump, requiring a forbidden extra step before tacking on the double toe loop. A major deduction.

"I felt really good until that triple lutz," she later commented. "I held back a little bit, waited too long to take the tap, overrotated, couldn't get out of it quick enough."

The rest of the program was beautiful and exciting, with exquisitely articulated jumps punctuating the choreography.

"I was pleased with the rest, but that triple lutz drove me crazy," she said.

She acknowledged the audience's ovation, but seemed furious at herself. "I waited so long!" she said to Frank Carroll, referring to the takeoff on the triple lutz. They watched the scores flash up: 5.4 to 5.6 for technical, 5.7 to 5.9 (from two judges) for presentation.

Two-time European champion Irina Slutskaya, in a royal-blue velvet costume with gold trim, and not a bit of makeup on her scrubbed-clean, pink-cheeked face, was next to skate. A powerful athlete, she always achieved great height and distance in her jumps.

The first element in her short program was the triple lutz, same as Michelle's, but she took a bad fall executing it, her entire body sliding over the ice. Other elements were powerfully performed, including a difficult "traveling" entrance into a triple-loop jump, and a double axel in which she extended one of her arms straight up into the air while rotating, also extremely difficult.

Although she rarely pointed her toes properly, that glaring stylistic flaw apparently didn't bother the judges. The fall, however, had been disastrous. Her technical marks were 5.1 to 5.4 for technical merit, 5.4 to 5.7 for presentation.

Chen-Lu, last year's runner-up to Michelle at Worlds and the champion the year before that, also skated the short program. Now twenty years old, her foot injury had flared up months ago, and her coach, Li Ming Zhu, explained that she hadn't been able to train properly. She was here only because it was a requirement to qualify for the '98 Olympics.

She was stunning in a sequinless black costume with shocking-pink trim, hair in an adult ponytail, and the audience welcomed her enthusiastically. As she skated to a jazz piece by Dave Brubeck, with choreography by Sandra Bezic, the first jump told the tale: she aborted her triple lutz, singled her double axel, missed other elements, and won scores ranging only from 3.0 to 4.0 for technical merit, 4.2 to 5.3 for presentation.

She unfortunately personified how fast and how far one could topple from the peak.

Tara remained in first place after the short. Coming in as U.S. champion had given her a lot of confidence, she said, and she had gained valuable experience during the last two competitions. But she had no illusions about the upcoming long program. "Everyone's going to be going for it," she noted.

The shocker of the evening was Vanessa Gusmeroli: she was in second place after the short! Maria Butyrskaya placed third, Michelle fourth, Irina Slutskaya sixth, Nicole Bobek eighth.

Michelle poured her heart out to Frank Carroll during the ride back from the arena. He has recalled how disappointed she was, how shocked and confused. Was her timing off? Had it been nerves? She'd been relatively calm and now she was angry. She felt she'd been so stupid, missing that jump, and went on berating herself until she stopped abruptly and realized what she was doing. Her friend Scott Hamilton was fighting for his life and she was despondent over *this*?

Carlo Fassi, whom she'd seen every day during training at Lake Arrowhead, was suddenly gone forever, and she was torturing herself over winning a skating championship?

Her view of her situation suddenly turned very down-to-earth and realistic.

CHAPTER NINETEEN

~~~

Back to Life

There was some good news for Michelle: she was positioned well in the skating order for the long program: fifth, following Vanessa Gusmeroli, Tara Lipinski, Krisztina Czako, and Maria Butyrskaya. Last to skate would be Irina Slutskaya, who'd taken a very bad fall during practice and required medical attention. It appeared she might have to withdraw.

Tara was no longer the newcomer with nothing to lose; now people's expectations were high, although she wasn't defending world champion. That honor still belonged to Michelle, and it wasn't impossible for her to move from fourth to first. Elvis Stojko had just done it! In the process, he made the record books by successfully completing the first quadruple-toe-triple-toe combination in world competition. And back in 1982, Elaine Zayak had moved from seventh place in the short to first place in the final standings, winning the world crown.

The outcome depended not only on how Michelle skated in the long, but on how the others performed as well. For one to climb the ladder, the occupant above must topple off the higher rung.

Nicole Bobek looked great during warm-up, her triple

lutz textbook perfect. It had been scarcely forty-eight hours since Carlo Fassi's demise, and she'd conducted herself with admirable restraint. She said she felt he was still with her, she just couldn't see him.

Her long program began superbly, with a wonderful double axel, but then she proceeded to double almost all of her triple jumps, and singled her final double axel. She'd obviously skated ultra-cautiously to avoid any mishap; it seemed she barely had the energy left to complete her program.

At the conclusion, she dropped to her knees, head bowed, hands clasped, and sobbed. She later revealed she'd wanted Mr. Fassi to know how much he meant to her, and that she "had tried."

She rose and took her bows, skated over to kiss-and-cry, and sat down sadly beside Christa Fassi and former Fassi star pupil Robin Cousins. Christa held her hand as Cousins tried to bolster her spirits. The scores didn't help: 4.1 to 4.9 for technical merit, 4.8 to 5.4 for presentation.

She knew she didn't skate well; it had been a tough two days. "I was glad to go out and do the best I could," she said.

Backstage, Tara Lipinski was sitting down, rocking back and forth. Then she lay back, closing her eyes.

Vanessa Gusmeroli, wearing red for her "circus"-themed program, fell on her opening jump, the triple flip, but followed with a series of solid triples and inventive spins. Her choreography, by Alan Schramm, was clever and effective, and the program registered strongly, but not as much as her short program. Nonetheless, the judges liked her: 5.3 to 5.7 for technical merit, 5.5 to 5.7 for presentation.

Lipinski, diminutive and delicate-looking in white, took to the ice next and was greeted by an ovation. Around her neck she wore a necklace engraved with the legend *Short But Good*. She'd solidly captured the imagination and interest of the public.

Skating again to the movie soundtracks of *Sense and Sensibility* and *Much Ado About Nothing*, she once again wove her spell, a graceful sprite performing without any mistakes. "I was a little nervous after being first in the short, but I think I really handled it well," she later said.

No matter how she placed, she would make the record books tonight as the first female to complete a triple-loop-triple-loop-jump combination in world competition. The difficulty factor arises from the fact that the skater has to leap up into the second jump directly after landing the first, which in the loop jump requires keeping the free leg forward rather than allowing it to swing back. A triumph of talent and technique, no question about it.

Four of the judges awarded her 5.9, three 5.8 for technical merit; for presentation, one 5.6, one 5.7, six 5.8s, one 5.9.

"Enjoy it!" Richard Callaghan told his beaming student in kiss-and-cry. So far, Tara was in first place with all nine judges.

Maria Butyrskaya, costumed once again in green, skated to the dramatic "Malagueña." The four-time Russian champion tended to land some of her jumps somewhat stiff-legged, and her movements weren't always smooth. The extension on her spirals left a lot to be desired as well, and tonight's ending on her program was sloppy.

But the judges liked her. She won 5.2 to 5.6 for technical merit, 5.5 to 5.8 for presentation.

As she conferred rinkside with Frank Carroll, Michelle Kwan's demeanor was dead serious, the expression on her face one of intense determination. Carroll reminded her of their conversation in the car; the goal was to *keep things in perspective*. After all, she realized, it wasn't as though she'd be sentenced to die if she didn't "perform."

Michelle's mind was fixed. Furthermore, she'd been preparing for this performance all year! "I said, 'Okay, let's have fun.' I just stepped on the ice and let myself fly."

But she didn't just fly ... she soared. From the moment she began her exquisite opening steps, there was nothing tentative in this performance. The initial triple-lutz-double-toe combination was a beauty, and ensuing jumps all worked; in terms of mature and charismatic presentation, she was, as Frank Carroll had told her she could and would be, "in a class by herself."

She *acted*, as well as skated, the Indian princess she portrayed. The only "mistake" she made was an omission, as she doubled her second triple lutz, and there were no deductions for it, but she followed it with a textbook-perfect triple salchow, then assumed her final back-bend position to coincide exactly with the final beat of music.

Michelle had sprung back to life! *She'd* been in charge tonight, and her demeanor afterward reflected her accomplishment. There were no tears, not from released tension or anything else. She'd gone out and done what she'd intended to do.

What did the judges think?

Backstage, Tara Lipinski's huge blue eyes were opened wide, having just observed Kwan's *coup de théâtre*. Surprise, concern, doubt, fear, and hope all seemed to flash across her face. She smiled instantly when she became aware that attention was focused on her.

Richard Callaghan stood close by as the results were tallied by the computers.

A certain scenario would have to unfold in order for Michelle to win: she'd not only have to place first in the long program, but Tara would have to finish third or lower.

Kwan's marks: 5.6 to 5.9 for technical merit; two 5.8s, seven 5.9s for presentation. So far, six judges placed her first, three put her in second.

Irina Slutskaya now took to the ice. No one could question her courage. Like Oksana Baiul back in '94, who skated her long program in the Olympics after colliding with another skater during practice and required painkilling injections, the injured Slutskaya had chosen not to withdraw.

The eighteen-year-old's program was, in effect, a series of powerful individual jumps and jump combinations, interspersed with spins and spin combinations, all performed without any significant relation to each other. The music was a wall of sound, the choreography, such as it was, was without any discernible theme. If this had been a group of competing opera singers instead of figure skaters, Slutskaya would have been one of those divas who hit a bravura series of high notes without any connecting melody in between.

Certainly her jumps were good and high, no doubt about it. The crowd liked her; she was one of their own. In the subjective and highly political world of figure-skating judges, many on the panel (which included no Americans) were apparently oblivious to Irina's shortcomings.

Three of them rated hers the outstanding free program of the evening, despite the flagrant bobble on her opening triple lutz; the nine judges were split on who should win first. In the end Michelle won the long program, but Tara had not slipped below second.

Lipinski became the youngest female world-figure-skating champion in history. "It's amazing! I'm still in shock, like I was at Nationals," she said. "It's great, I love it. Everything fell into place." She acknowledged that she'd worked hard and had been confident, and that feeling that way had been "a big thing." Her next dream: winning Olympic gold at Nagano.

With Kwan in a final second place, Vanessa Gusmeroli in third, and Slutskaya fourth, Tara had toppled Sonja Henie's seventy-year-old record and established one of her own.

Lipinski knew who Sonja was, and acknowledged that being the youngest was a great accomplishment. "But whatever age you are," she said, "you're happy with what you get."

As for Michelle? She had won her own triumph: the battle against herself. She'd gotten her act back together, proven that she could still do it. And this time she'd done it for all the right reasons! "To tell you the truth, this is the only time I've enjoyed skating this year!" she exclaimed. Her attitude had been strictly no-nonsense: "We're here, *skate*! That's it."

CHAPTER TWENTY

The Best Is Yet to Come

How will Michelle feel if she doesn't win the Olympics? "I guess I'd be disappointed," she has said. "But you have to learn to cope and be happy and enjoy life. A lot of things aren't going to go your way."

She said she'd learned that the skater who wins all the time may be great and powerful, but the skater who has fallen and been injured, and who can get up again and stand and fight, is the one she admired most.

In the best of all possible worlds, the idea was not to let skating become Michelle's identity, to only permit it to define who she was and what she was supposed to do away from the ice.

In 1998, she will be a high-school senior. She has expressed interest in attending Harvard and then law school. She also has given thought to pursuing a career in television, or becoming a district attorney.

With success on the ice coming her way at such an early age, Michelle obviously has plenty of time to make a "comeback," absurd though it seems to be talking like this at the age of seventeen! After all, Michelle hadn't placed last in the '97 Nationals and Worlds—she'd won Silver, and at Worlds had won the long program!

Many parallels to Michelle's experiences exist in other sports. For example, tennis legend Boris Becker was aghast on hearing the angst expressed by friends and fans after he suffered a defeat. "Hey! I only lost a tennis match; nobody died!" he exclaimed. A month after his record-setting victory at the 1997 Masters, twenty-one-year-old Tiger Woods found himself struggling in a tournament. After the first round, he was not even among the top-ten players. His legendary swing, which had recently earned him a record $21 million contract to represent American Express, had suddenly become "too steep." The following month Woods and Greg Norman were both far behind in a tournament. "I knew what I was doing wrong," explained Woods, "but I couldn't stop it."

This is no different from when a figure skater suddenly finds her free leg swinging too wide, or when her timing is off, and a key jump has vanished! Setbacks occur; it's inevitable even for the greatest champions.

For Michelle, the climb back up is hardly impossible. Why look at the proverbial glass as half-empty when it is half-full? To quote Madonna: "If you just keep on going, put your mind to something, you can accomplish anything."

Michelle has developed, in her own words, a much "looser" attitude about her skating; she understands that mistakes she's made in the past needn't be repeated in the future.

And her accomplishments to date are beyond formidable. How many can say they've won both the U.S. Nationals and World Figure Skating Championships? And have done so by the age of fifteen!

Her collection to date of Gold Medals could fill a den.

(Sonja Henie actually set aside a room in her home especially for her trophies and medals, and called it her "Inspiration Room.") And what were the odds that an eight-year-old watching the Olympics on television would one day become friends with and skate with the young man whose accomplishments had fired her imagination? This, too, had come to pass for Michelle: Brian Boitano was one of her stalwart supporters.

In the summer of 1997, they would star together in "Skating Romance III—Love Is in the Air," a unique presentation on ice. It was literally a dream come true for Kwan.

Athletes in other fields had become fans of Michelle's. Michelle Kwan on a baseball diamond? That was one image that certainly had never occurred to anyone (except perhaps her brother, Ron), but she was front and center in early June at the Chicago White Sox–Baltimore Orioles game in Chicago. She was nervous—she had to throw the first pitch. It was "a long throw from the pitcher's place to home plate." She wasn't sure if she'd thrown a strike, but White Sox third baseman Chris Snopek told her she'd done a good job.

Michelle also utilized her prominence as an athlete to further causes she believed in: she was featured in a TV special, *Alien Vacation!,* which dealt with the treatment of animals and endangered species.

All but forgotten, after the dizzying hoopla surrounding the 1997 Nationals, Worlds, etc., was a significant victory Michelle had achieved back in December 1996. Kwan had competed against the skater she considered "the best I've ever seen." Michelle said that in her wildest dreams, she'd never envisioned them vying against each other for a title.

It was Kwan v. Kristi Yamaguchi (and others) at a pro-am event in Boston. Kristi said she had felt a bit like the underdog, coming back to the rigid rules of an Olympic division–style system of judging. A professional for five years (and nine years Michelle's senior), she was the undisputed queen of the pro skaters. Michelle had the utmost respect for Kristi as a skater and a person.

It was a close contest, but Michelle won. She skated her "Pocahontas" routine for the long program and infused the performance with strength and exquisite sensitivity. Afterward, she said she felt she'd *become* the character, and joked, "Where's my John Smith?"

Neither Kristi nor Michelle had thought of the competition as a showdown between them—although they both had given it their all. It had certainly offered purists the opportunity to simultaneously appreciate two of the skating world's greatest contemporary talents, and neither artist suffered in comparison.

Having to make a choice between them was the equivalent of deciding between Tiffany and Cartier; one couldn't go wrong either way!

There is an attractive new maturity in Michelle's demeanor; even her speaking voice is pitched lower. Her femininity is blossoming; a more experienced and sophisticated outlook becomes her.

Numerous athletes have succeeded in regaining a title. Elvis Stojko, fourth in the '96 Worlds after taking a spill, won back the title in '97. "To be able to come back . . . and push away everything and still believe in myself, that's what makes it special," he said.

Todd Eldredge had the same experience. "Nobody can win every time," he noted. "Enjoy it while you have it, but stay focused on what got you there in the first place: training and hard work."

Of her rivalry with Tara Lipinski, Michelle had this to say: "We don't hate each other." She even had words of advice for her competitor: Tara should keep things in perspective and enjoy herself.

Meanwhile, others are always watching and measuring opportunity—Michelle and Tara are not the only competitors!

At a recent Harvard University Jimmy Fund performance, an eleven-year-old skating prodigy named Patrice Ann McDonough brought down the house. In looks and style, she is a startling combination of Michelle Kwan and Tara Lipinski. Already she has mastered the triple lutz, and spins like a top.

To avoid the possibility of ever having to award the World Championship to a five-year-old who is able to jump a quadruple toe, a rule has been passed that from now on a competitor must be at least fifteen years old to enter world competition.

Michelle and Tara conceivably could be competing against each other for years. By the 2002 Olympics— slated for Salt Lake City, Utah—Michelle will be only twenty-one, Tara nineteen.

Frank Carroll views Kwan and Lipinski as two wonderful skaters with completely different styles. He has gone so far as to say, though, that Michelle is "more able to give something from the heart."

Tara's coach, Richard Callaghan, describes both young

women as great champions. Who will win the next contest? "It depends on who's better on a particular day."

Tara and Michelle will compete once again in late October 1997 at a site filled with memories for Michelle: the Joe Louis Arena in Detroit, Michigan. It was there that Kwan had triumphed in Nationals back in 1994, when an injured Nancy Kerrigan observed the competition from a private box high above the arena.

Michelle will enter this Champion Series contest as reigning two-time champion. The event will kick off the competition-filled 1997–1998 season, culminating in February with the Winter Olympic Games in Nagano, Japan, followed a month later by the World Championships.

As far as anyone knows, Frank Carroll has no plans for Michelle to portray another femme fatale during the Olympic season. All he has said is that beautiful music has been chosen that no skater has ever used before. Michelle's program "will be different and exciting, another movement for her to explore."

On June 21, 1997, in New York City, Kwan dazzled a packed Madison Square Garden audience as one of the stars (along with Tara Lipinski, Elvis Stojko, Brian Boitano, Nancy Kerrigan, Rudy Galindo, Todd Eldredge, and Viktor Petrenko) of Tom Collins's Campbell's Soups 1997 Tour of World Figure Skating Champions. Her friend Oksana Baiul had rejoined the tour, and Michelle and the others were in full support of Baiul's efforts to begin anew. After all, that's what life is about: helping friends to realize their potential.

Performing to "On My Own" from *Les Misérables*, and then to Louis Armstrong's classic rendition of "What a Wonderful World," Michelle was skating better than ever, not only technically but as a performer. In musicians' parlance, she skated with *soul*.

"She has developed into a mature and beautiful champion before our eyes," says Jo Jo Starbuck, herself one of figure skating's most beautiful and accomplished champions. "Michelle has grown into an exquisite young woman on the ice; there are such subtleties to her skating. Doing 'On My Own,' it's so obvious how much she cares about the meaning of that song. She skates with such passion! There are so many special moments—her hand positions, the position of her free leg. So much thought has gone into it and the performance emerges as a work of art!"

Tara Lipinski, who turned fifteen on June 10, didn't disappoint her fans on that evening either. Her opening appearance was skated to Doris Day's classic rendition of "Qué Sera, Sera." The lyric offers insight, one can assume, into Tara's current state of mind: "Whatever will be, will be."

"I've learned that winning isn't about miracles on ice. It's all about training," Michelle has observed.

She has certainly earned the respect and affection of millions of people throughout the world, demonstrating a healthy resilience in a tough and demanding profession.

Teenagers are among her most ardent fans. One in particular, Louisa Khettav, who works part-time in the Forest Hills branch of the New York Public Library, summed it up: "You're doing a book about Michelle Kwan? I *love* her!" Why? "Because I can tell she skates to express *what* she is and *who* she is, she's not skating just for the judges." Louisa's dark eyes are sparkling with enthusiasm as she continues. "That's *important*. You can tell she's someone *special*."

APPENDIX

Selected Skating Terms

JUMPS

AXEL: Axel Paulsen, a Norwegian, devised this jump, in which the skater takes off from a forward outside edge, revolves one and a half times in the air, and lands on the opposite foot on a back outside edge. The double axel requires two and a half revolutions in the air; the triple axel, three and a half revolutions. Because of the forward outside-edge takeoff, it is often considered the most treacherous jump.

FLIP: The skater usually enters from a forward three turn (wherein the skater by pivoting on the toe pick, smoothly switches from the outside to the inside edge), remains on the back inside edge, reaches back with the free leg, taps the blade's toe pick into the ice, and vaults into the air, revolving in a counterclockwise direction, and landing on the opposite foot on a back outside edge. The double and triple flips require, respectively, two and three revolutions in the air.

LOOP JUMP: This jump calls for the skater to lift off from a back outside edge, turn one, two, or three revolutions in the air, and land on the same foot on a back outside edge.

LUTZ: Created by Alois Lutz, an Austrian, this jump requires the skater, on a back outside edge, to reach back with the free leg, "tap" the blade's toe pick into the ice, and vault himself into the air, revolving in a counterclockwise direction and landing on a back outside edge. The double and triple lutzes require, respectively, two and three revolutions in the air.

SALCHOW: Named for its creator, Sweden's Ulrich Salchow, this jump requires taking off from the back inside edge, revolving once, twice, or three times, in the air, and landing on the opposite foot on a back outside edge.

TOE LOOP: Considered the "easiest" of the triple jumps, the skater takes off from a back outside edge, tapping the free-leg toe pick into the ice, vaults into the air, and lands on a back outside edge. The upper-body position enables the skater to "wind up" most easily for this jump; a quadruple (four turns in the air) toe loop has been successfully landed in competition.

Note: Scientific tests have determined that it takes 40 percent more physical effort to jump a triple than a double.

SPINS

Done properly and sustained correctly, spins require even more energy than jumps. They're not over in a split second and can evolve mid-spin into many different positions.

CAMEL SPIN: Requires the skater to assume the arabesque position, the free leg extended in back at a right angle to the surface of the ice. This spin can be done forward, backward, and as part of a jump (the "flying camel"), landing in the camel-spin position. The Beillmann Camel (popularized by Switzerland's Denise Beillmann) is a dramatic variation, in which the skater reaches back, grabs the skate blade of her free leg, and raises her leg to optimum height over her head while spinning.

LAYBACK SPIN: Primarily (although not exclusively) a ladies' spin; the skater bends backward while spinning. The deeper the arch in the back, the more difficult and effective the spin. The free leg should not be held close to the body, which many skaters do because it's easier, but it is not a proper position.

SIT SPIN: Invented by America's Jackson Haines and originally called the "Jackson Haines Spin," this element requires that the skater spin in a sitting position. There are many variations, including the "flying" sit spin (jumping up into the air, assuming for a fraction of a second a sitting position at the peak of the jump, and landing in the sit spin), an "axel" sit spin, a "change" sit spin (changing from one foot to the other while spinning), etc.

Caption List for Photos

Inside front cover, top:

AMERICA'S BEST: Michelle and Tara at the 1997 World Championships. (Kwan will be seventeen, Lipinski fifteen on entering the 1998 Olympics in Nagano, Japan.)

Inside front cover, bottom:

Kwan *enjoys* performing for audiences.

First page of book, top:

Perfect form: a back sit spin (1993 U.S. Championships). Michelle was thirteen.

First page of book, bottom:

A layback spin (1995 Skate America). Michelle was fifteen.

Second page of book, top:

Victory at the 1996 World Championships in Edmonton, Alberta. Michelle was four months shy of her sixteenth birthday.

Second-to-last page of book, top:

Midair in a double axel (two and a half revolutions).

Second-to-last page of book, bottom:

Mesmerizing in her "Taj Mahal"–inspired long

program (Paris, 1996), Kwan won the Lalique Trophy.

Last page of book:

> With best friend and confidante, sister Karen, who is two years older than Michelle.

Inside back cover:

> Once a champion, always a champion.

About the Author

Edward Z. Epstein, whose eighteen published books include biographies of Mia Farrow, Paul Newman and Joanne Woodward, Lucille Ball, and Academy Award–winning actress Jennifer Jones, is also a dedicated figure skater and a former Middle Atlantic States Novice champion.

His articles on figure skating have appeared in, among other periodicals, *Scandinavian Review*, New York's *Sunday News* magazine, and *Cutting Edge*. In the winter of 1993, he helped organize a festival of Sonja Henie's films for New York's Museum of Modern Art and wrote the official museum notes for the series.

He has worked with and written articles on the lives of, among others, Natalie Wood and Ava Gardner. His play based on the life of Ms. Gardner has been optioned by producer David Brown.

Mr. Epstein, a graduate of New York University, is a native New Yorker.

*The Dazzling Rise of
a Young Country Star*

DREAM
COME
TRUE

THE LEANN RIMES STORY
by
Jo Sgammato

Who is this singer with the incredible voice, the youngest
artist ever nominated for a Country Music Association
Award, and winner of the Grammy Award for Best New
Artist? Find out all this and more in this heartwarming
story, complete with four pages of color photos!

Published by Ballantine Books.
Available at your local bookstore.